4+

D0910253

WITHDRAWN

CLOSER TO HOME

# ❧ CLOSER TO HOME

*Writers and Places in England, 1780–1830*

ROGER SALE

HARVARD UNIVERSITY PRESS

Cambridge, Massachusetts, and London, England   1986

*Library of Congress Cataloging-in-Publication Data*

Sale, Roger.
  Closer to home.

  Includes index.
  Contents: Circumstances alter occasions—George
Crabbe—Jane Austen—William Cobbett—John Clare—
William Wordsworth.
  1. English literature—19th century—History and criticism.  2. Setting (literature)  3. Local color in literature.  4. Regionalism in literature.  5. England in
literature  6. English literature—18th century—History
and criticism.  7. Authors, English—Homes and
haunts.  8. Literary landmarks—England.  I. Title.
PR468.S47S35  1986      820'.9'007      86-12067
ISBN 0-674-13625-X

*Designed by Gwen Frankfeldt*

For Paul Alpers

And for my part, if only one allow
The care my laboring spirits take in this,
He is to me a theater large enow,
And his applause only sufficient is,
All my respect is bent but to his brow;
This is my all, and all I am is his.

—Samuel Daniel, *Musophilus*

# CONTENTS

CLOSER TO HOME

# I

## ❧ CIRCUMSTANCES ALTER OCCASIONS

IN THE HISTORY of English literature the years 1780–1830 are conceded to be one of the periods of greatest change, and a crucial aspect of the change is a shift of attention from the general to the particular or individual. In *Rasselas* Johnson's Imlac commands the poet "to examine, not the individual, but the species," to "disregard present laws and opinions, and rise to general and transcendental truths"; sixty years later Keats writes that souls gain "a bliss peculiar to each one's individual existence," and only "by the medium of a world like this." In Keats's time the "world like this" comes to be the immediate environment of a writer or character, and in literature place has a larger role than ever before in shaping lives—including, for the first time, the lives of children.

My concern is with place, and the way places are rendered, in the work of five authors—Crabbe, Austen, Cobbett, Clare, and Wordsworth. Their writings are dissimilar in style, tone, temper, subject, and genre; what they have in common is primarily their difference from earlier writers in the way they create places. Since this is the "Romantic period" and only one of the five is a Romantic, it may seem that my selection does injustice to the literature that is understood to lie at the heart of the period. In actuality, if injustice is done, I think it is by the label "Romantic period." The term, meant to be descriptive, has become honorific, with the result that Romantic authors receive greater attention than others of their time and are presumed to be more worthy of attention. While my main aim is to look freshly at these five writers, I admit I have chosen them partly because they allow me to shift the emphasis away from the "Romantic period" and toward a sense of great variety that defies a single label.

I have spent considerable time in Crabbe's Aldeburgh, Clare's Helpston, Wordsworth's Lake District, and Austen's Hampshire, and have taken some of Cobbett's rural rides. Though the results of those visits do not receive much space in these essays, the book in fact began when I first learned what such pilgrimages could yield—in D. H. Lawrence's Eastwood, in the Gainsborough that George Eliot made into St. Ogg's, and in Hardy's Wessex. Places change, to be sure: Egdon Heath is now a conifer forest, and Dickens' London no longer exists. But there are places, rural ones especially, that retain much of the quality they had in earlier times and help one "see" the writers or their characters in a different light. Even if all that a visit does is bring home, or bring together, bits of knowledge that might have remained unexamined, something is gained. Some years ago, for instance, I visited Fawley, a village in southern Oxfordshire whose name Hardy gave Jude as his surname, and the spot nearby where Jude strains to see the spires of Christminster. My visit to the village (called Marygreen in the novel) confirmed Hardy's description of it as forlorn and isolated. Yet Hardy's grandmother was from there, and Hardy had gone there not only in the 1890s to gain his bearings for *Jude the Obscure* but in the 1860s, accompanied by another woman, to see his sister. The place where Jude sees Christminster is also the place where Jude and Arabella live when they are married, and where the gibbet was that hanged the man who murdered his family, and where odd meetings take place late in the novel. The visit helped me see why the place was resonant for Hardy and what led him to take his strange and powerful novel in the directions he did. It was forays like this into the places at the heart of some great English fiction that led me to wonder how and when specific places had become important in English literature.

In the nineteenth century there is a particularization, often a localization, in the way places are conceived and described, and a conviction that place plays an important part in people's lives. If these characteristics do not loom as large in the literature of this century, they are still much in evidence, and we all know easily and instinctively the ways of thinking that underlie them. Place in Shakespeare, by contrast, is created not to describe particular places precisely or to root characters in places. There are particulars, of course, in his descriptions:

> *Duncan.*   This castle hath a pleasant seat; the air
> Nimbly and sweetly recommends itself
> Unto our gentle senses.
> *Banquo.*                          This guest of summer,
> The temple-haunting martlet, does approve,
> By his loved mansionry, that the heaven's breath
> Smells wooingly here: no jutty, frieze,
> Buttress, nor coign of vantage, but this bird
> Hath made his pendent bed, and procreant cradle:
> Where they most breed and haunt, I have observ'd
> The air is delicate.

The stage direction reads "Inverness." It is the name of an actual place, but only a name. The air around Macbeth's castle, and the martlets with their nests, are all there as details, not because martlets ever bred in Inverness Castle but because Duncan is to be killed there on this day of his arrival. Thus St. Albans, Towton, Barnet, Bosworth Field, Wakefield, and Shrewesbury are all named as places of battle in the history plays, and what Shakespeare does to make place and action harmonious is to offer battle language at each place. Before the end of the eighteenth century, place in literature tends to be generalized, a kind of place. Pastoral place, court place, Eden, Renaissance Italy, ancient Rome, and Troy, all had language which writers inherited, and that vocabulary was all that was needed to designate the place or kind of place in question.

The actuality of the place, and what can be called the realism or verifiability of the details, do not really matter. Here, for instance, is the opening of Ben Jonson's "To Penshurst":

> Thou art not, Penshurst, built to envious show
> Of touch, or marble; nor canst boast a row

Of polished pillars, or a roof of gold:
  Thou hast no lanthern, whereof tales are told;
Or stairs, or courts; but stand'st an ancient pile,
  And these grudged at, art reverenced the while.
Thou joy'st in better marks, of soil, of air,
  Of wood, of water: therein thou art fair.
Thou hast thy walkes for health, as well as sport:
  Thy Mount, to which the dryads do resort,
Where Pan, and Bacchus their high feasts have made,
  Beneath the broad beech, and the chestnut shade;
The taller tree, which of a nut was set,
  At his great birth, where all the muses met.

A visitor to Penshurst today can see that indeed it was not built for envious show, and it has woods, water, and walks, perhaps for health as much as sport; that it is an ancient pile, built in the fourteenth century, almost three centuries before Jonson's poem; that its great hall is one anyone might reverence. So the visitor might conclude there is no great difference, in the way place is rendered, between this Jonson poem and Hardy's Egdon Heath or Lawrence's Breadalby in *Women in Love.*

Yet Jonson's is a generalized place into which particularized and actual details are fit. "To Penshurst" is the first of a little sub-genre called country house poems, but its means, its devices, are quite traditional and are governed by an inherited sense of literary decorum. The muses met at Penshurst when Philip Sidney was born, and Pan and Bacchus make their feasts on Penshurst's mount—these are obvious inventions which Jonson asks us to understand in the same way we understand that Penshurst offers no display of marble, and in the same way we understand the carp later on in the poem who run eagerly into fish nets, as Jonson adapts a passage from Juvenal. These details could never have been verified, but the poem does not allow for the distinction we might wish to make between details verifiable and unverifiable. All the details are employed without regard to their actual source to celebrate a place that exists in Jonson's mind. Obviously Jonson would not wish to praise Penshurst for qualities the Sidneys would not wish to be praised for, and he would

4

not have said that James I had visited Penshurst if in fact he had not. These facts, though, are in the poem to help create a society in which high people and low people, the human and the natural and the mythic, meet and live harmoniously. Whether such a society existed is not Jonson's concern, and if the details of Penshurst Place can offer Jonson some material for his poem, they can never dictate the poem's terms, which are ideal. Thus Raymond Williams, in *The City and the Country*, can gain little when he writes that "To Penshurst" is less candid, less revealing of actual life at country houses, than Marvell is in "Upon Appleton House." Marvell's poem is more extravagant than Jonson's, much longer and much more willing to seem to lose control of its direction. It too creates an ideal, however, even as it uses the real; "realism," in the sense of "being revealing, telling all," has no part in the aim of either poet.

During the eighteenth century we can see the process at work whereby earlier descriptions of places came to be set aside and misunderstood. Poets, critics, philosophers, architects, painters, and landscape designers all thought they had begun something exciting and new, a movement or series of movements that would put buildings like Penshurst and poems like Jonson's far behind. The umbrella term here is "picturesque," and while it covers a variety of things and ideas, all can be distinguished both from earlier places and descriptions of places and from the places created in the literature of 1780–1830. As the word implies, the picturesque has to do with pictures; and as John Barrell notes at the outset of *The Idea of Landscape and the Sense of Place*, there is no term in English for land seen *visually* and not also seen *pictorially*. There may be details in "To Penshurst" that can be called visual, but they and the others are not composed so that we can see them together, as in a picture. The Reverend William Gilpin, a tireless eighteenth-century traveler and enthusiast of the picturesque, calls works like "To Penshurst," with some derision, "a painted survey, a mere map," because it uses no perspective, no pictorial elements. What one finds in the paintings of Claude Lorrain and Salvator Rosa, in the landscapes designed by William Kent and Capability Brown, and in many

English poems but especially Thomson's *Seasons* are composed places, understood pictorially, of a kind that earlier literature shows only traces of here and there.

But if from their own perspective the creators of the picturesque were establishing a new ideal, we can from our later perspective see how much the picturesque is governed by an *idea* of place which keeps places generalized even when named, when in fact the locale is one place and not another. If the means, and the ideals, of "To Penshurst" are different from those that govern scenes in the *Seasons*, in both cases the means and the ideals could be, and in fact were, used by others when writing about different places. One can move from a Thomson scene to one by Akenside, or Gray or Goldsmith or Brown or Kent, and see the same principles at work throughout. One cannot do that when moving from Wordsworth to Austen or to Clare.

Here is one of the most famous of literary picturesque scenes, that of Hagley Park, in Thomson's "Spring":

> Meantime you gain the height, from whose fair brow
> The bursting prospect spreads immense around;
> And, snatched o'er hill and dale, and wood and lawn,
> And verdant field, and darkening heath between,
> And villages embosomed soft in trees,
> And spiry towns by surging columns marked
> Of household smoke, your eye excursive roams—
> Wide-stretching from the Hall in whose kind haunt
> The hospitable Genius lingers still,
> To where the broken landscape, by degrees
> Ascending, roughens into rigid hills
> O'er which the Cambrian mountains, like far clouds
> That skirt the blue horizon, dusky rise.

It is doubtful if the scene Thomson describes was there in the fourteenth century, when Hagley Hall was built. It is an ideal landscape, and its ideal is an eighteenth-century ideal. In the passage, and presumably in the prospect, all is arranged, as John Barrell shows in his account of the lines, so that the eye first takes in the prospect as an overwhelming scene, and then is

6

"snatched" to make its way along a series of horizontal planes, working from foreground to background, down to woods and lawns, out to darkening heath and village smoke, back quickly to the hall before looking out to the hills and mountains in the distance. This is the action of the passage because it is the way the prospect was planned by the designer of Hagley's landscape, using principles derived from the paintings of Claude. The appeal of these picturesque scenes retained its hold for many years. Of my five writers, only Cobbett, whose bearings were never literary-aesthetic, did not grow up imbibing the picturesque; it is discussed explicitly in *Sense and Sensibility* and *The Prelude*, it is part of what Crabbe reacts against in *The Village*, and it is consciously and unconsciously imitated in Clare's early poetry.

The picturesque has two major appeals: the first and most obvious is to the eye, to see a picture in a landscape; the second is to private or solitary experience as opposed to the social ideal offered by poems like "To Penshurst" and "Upon Appleton House" in the seventeenth century. In Thomson's description of Hagley's prospect, the only suggestions of any people at all are in the distance, "villages embosomed soft in trees" and "spiry towns by surging columns marked / Of household smoke." The trouble with the picturesque, if that is the word for it, is that it was a taste that could easily become satisfied and jaded. Nevertheless the picturesque remained part of the air people breathed well into the nineteenth century.

A transitional figure is William Cowper, who himself remained a solid eighteenth-century topographical poet and occasional satirist, but in ways that endeared him to some of the most sensitive souls of the next two generations, such as the great clergy daughters, Austen and the Brontë sisters, who were like him in being in but not of the countryside, and John Clare, who could always spot an impostor and knew that Cowper was genuine. After he retired to Olney, in Buckinghamshire, Cowper was rooted and local, but in the 1780s his bearings are those of Thomson and the picturesque:

> Thou know'st my praise of nature most sincere,
> And that my raptures are not conjur'd up

To serve occasions of poetic pomp,
But genuine, and art partner of them all.

Cowper appeals to his companion to attest that he is not just another picturesque gentleman tourist, but the passage that follows could hardly be cited as evidence until the end:

Here Ouse, slow winding through a level plain
Of spacious meads with cattle sprinkled o'er,
Conducts the eye along the sinuous course
Delighted. There, fast rooted in their bank,
Stand, never overlook'd, our fav'rite elms,
That screen the herdsman's solitary hut;
While far beyond, and overthwart the stream
That, as with molten glass, inlays the vale,
The sloping land recedes into the clouds;
Displaying on its varied side the grace
Of hedge-row beauties numberless, square tow'r,
Tall spire, from which the sound of cheerful bells
Just undulates upon the list'ning ear,
Groves, heaths, and smoking villages remote.
Scenes must be beautiful, which, daily view'd,
Please daily, and whose novelty survives
Long knowledge and the scrutiny of years.

The river conducts the eye from foreground to background, from cattle to elms, the hedgerow, church tower, and village smoke; in 1785, when Cowper wrote this, it must have seemed there was little he could add to this kind of composition. The difference comes primarily at the end. Cowper loves what he sees not because it conforms to aesthetic principles but because it is his, and "Scenes must be beautiful, which, daily view'd, / Please daily." There are no standards for beauty in Olney, and nothing here is to be compared aesthetically with anyplace else. His is local experience accumulated over the "scrutiny of years," and Cowper knows the herdsman's hut is there even though the elms hide it. Give Cowper a scene and he will describe it in traditional and generalized terms, but *The Task*—though it is a rambling poem and an indifferent whole indeed—is one of the first literary works about what a man knows because he knows a place in its daily and seasonal activities. As a work of transition, it belongs alongside its quiet and steadying contemporary, Gilbert White's *Natural History of Selborne*.

Finally I would like to look at what may be the most famous place of all in these years, the river Stour and Willy Nott's cottage in John Constable's *The Hay-Wain*. Constable's large canvases are so much everyone's image of the typical English countryside that it is easy to overlook the fact that they were not this for Constable, who never sought the typical, or the ideal, or means of generalization. He was rooted in a few square miles on the border between Suffolk and Essex; he said many times that this land of his childhood had chosen him and made him a painter. Michael Rosenthal, one of Constable's recent critics, compares *The Hay-Wain* with Claude's *Aeneas at Delos*, and the comparison is like one between Cowper and Thomson, though Constable moves much further from Claude than Cowper does from Thomson. *Aeneas at Delos* is a typical Claude and needs little describing; it is a series of horizontal planes leading from small figures in the foreground to the light source at the horizon. The temple is on the right, while its equivalent in *The Hay-Wain*, Willy Nott's cottage, is on the left; the tree just left of center in Claude is just right of center in Constable.

One must, however, be deeply devoted to the idea that Constable's painting "derives" from something other than the place on the river Stour in order to follow Rosenthal's comparison, so much more particularized and unyielding of generalization is Constable's composition. His planes are not distinctly horizontal; the elms tend to enclose the space, the river leads the eye into the distance to no apparent consequence, the farthest field and the forest yield no compositional resting point. *The Hay-Wain* does not seem composed in the picturesque sense, and Constable chose to paint this scene not because therein nature contrived to offer picturesque effects but because it had chosen him, at an age when he could not refuse it.

Not being able to see *The Hay-Wain* as a "bursting prospect" spreading "immense around," one begins to examine individual elements in the picture and then starts asking questions. Is the dog barking, or just staring at a familiar human scene? Is the boy fishing with skilled care, or is he a beginner, about to get his line tangled in the bushes? What are those men doing, no hay in the wain, no place for the horses to go? Is one of the men giving orders, or is his a ritual gesture, calmly made and clearly understood? Wordsworth once complained of Walter Scott that in his landscapes he was always the artist whose work was proudly on display. One could not say that of Constable, who is absorbed in a scene he knows so well and paints so lovingly that he does not need to comment or proclaim his virtuosity. Personally he very much needed to be made a member of the Royal Academy, and his adult professional life seems divided into the years before and the years after he was named. As a painter, though, he seems to need no one else, and this may have been why the Academy put him off for so long. He knows that this is the river Stour, but I'm not sure we can tell if this is a river at all. He knows the wain may be in the water to let the horses cool their hooves and fetlocks, or, more likely, and I quote another who spent his life in the Constable country, "to keep the wood of the rims from shrinking and allowing the 'fellies' or segments to work loose on each other and from the spokes." Presumably Constable knows what the dog is doing and how skilled the lad is at fishing, but he knows so completely and is absorbed in his scene so unselfconsciously that he does not feel the need to explain.

This is what it means to be in a local, particularized place. I offer it here not to imply that the places we will be looking at are like Constable's; of my five authors, the only one he resembles is Clare, who is eager and lyric in his absorption in his places, in contrast to Constable's appearance of calm repose. Rather, Constable summons us on one of the ways we are going, and we are going to go in five directions. Constable gives us "local" and "particular" in a way that is different from the ways of the generalized and ideal landscapes of earlier painting and poetry. But if one thinks of, say, Jane Austen's portrayal of Lyme in *Persuasion*, Dorothy Wordsworth's slow accumulating way of showing us life at Dove Cottage in her journals, Coleridge's description of the waterfall on Buttermere Hause Fell in his notebooks, Scott's quiet account of the married life of Reuben and Jeanie at Knockartlitie at the end of *The Heart of Midlothian*, Shelley's delineation of sky and life under the water in "Ode to the West Wind," one senses in what varied ways place became particular or local for writers in these fifty years. It is a transitional period, to be sure; these places, and most of those in the following chapters, are not "home places" as the term came to be used later. But we are getting closer to home.

# II

## ❧ GEORGE CRABBE

CRABBE WAS born in 1754, nine years before Cobbett, sixteen before Wordsworth, twenty-one before Austen, and thirty-eight before Clare. He always wrote in heroic couplets, always seemed a latter-day Augustan. His two best volumes, *The Borough* (1810) and *Tales in Verse* (1812), were very popular, and shortly after their publication Crabbe sold John Murray the rights to all his work for the handsome figure of £3000. Poetry itself was enormously popular at this time, and on the register of contemporary recognition Crabbe ranked a remarkable third, behind Scott and Byron.

But the reputations of Scott and Crabbe both became at risk as Byron's star rose, and although Crabbe's *Tales from the Hall* was well received when it was published in 1819, one edition was enough to exhaust the public's interest. By the time he died in 1832, he was well on his way to being forgotten. Later, when the label "Romantic period" was given us, the movement's first important dates were those of Blake's *Songs of Innocence and Experience* (1789 and 1793) and Wordsworth and Coleridge's *Lyrical Ballads* (1798). By the time this label was affixed, late in the last century, there was no fuss about what to "do" with Crabbe, since he could safely be ignored, and the Augustan label let him slide back into the eighteenth century. In one of the leading anthologies of English literature he is found under "Types of Eighteenth Century Poetry" and represented only by Book I of *The Village*, the poem that first gave him recognition

13

in 1783. Once he is placed in that period, it is perhaps inevitable that he is best known for the poem that Edmund Burke and Samuel Johnson liked, though it is far from his best or most representative. Reordering is in order.

Actually, if Burke had not taken notice of Crabbe, it is likely that he would never have gained any reputation at all. He was born in the fishing village of Aldeburgh, on the North Sea coast, the son of a minor customs inspector who was often impoverished and often drunk. The elder Crabbe loved poetry, though, and introduced his son to *Paradise Lost* and Edward Young's *Night Thoughts*, and sent him to school some miles away, in Bungay, where the boy learned to write poetry. That was the extent of the father's ambition and resources, however. So the son came home and for years struggled to survive as an apothecary's apprentice in various Suffolk towns, and afterwards, back in Aldeburgh, as the parish-appointed apothecary to the poor. Crabbe seems to have gone on writing, but his income was seldom more than that of those to whom he ministered. In 1782 he went to London, desperate to find someone who would take notice of *The Village*; he had enough learning to make himself a genuine heir to a tradition, but if he failed to gain attention, he had only a life of poverty to look forward to. Fortunately Burke did take notice, and not only was the poem published but Burke arranged for Crabbe's ordination in the Church of England. All was not simple smooth sailing after that, when Crabbe returned to Aldeburgh and discovered what his Redeemer had meant by a prophet's having honor except in his own country. The Aldeburgh parishioners were reluctant to accept the former apothecary as their spiritual leader, and Crabbe left for good, to accept two livings in the Vale of Belvoir, on the border of Lincolnshire and Leicestershire. He had been engaged for over a decade and now could get married and start a family. Except for a dull poem called "The Newspaper," he published nothing for over twenty years, and during that time no one need have thought any more about him than about any rural minister who read, wrote, stayed aloof, and disturbed no one's peace.

Crabbe's silence of two decades has never been explained, but one reason may be that he had to learn to write a different poetry, or a different version of the same kind of poetry. *The Village* has about it a good deal of combative vitality, born of Crabbe's sense that although many had written about country life in the eighteenth century, and Goldsmith had indeed addressed himself to the plight of the rural poor, none really knew that country and that poverty as he did, first hand:

> Lo! where the heath, with withering brake grown o'er,
> Lends the light turf that warms the neighbouring poor;
> From thence a length of burning sand appears,
> Where the thin harvest waves its wither'd ears;
> Rank weeds, that every art and care defy,
> Reign o'er the land, and rob the blighted rye:
> There thistles stretch their prickly arms afar,
> And to the ragged infant threaten war;
> There poppies nodding, mock the hope of toil;
> There the blue bugloss paints the sterile soil;
> Hardy and high, above the slender sheaf,
> The slimy mallow waves her silky leaf;
> O'er the young shoot the charlock throws a shade,
> And clasping tares cling round the sickly blade;
> With mingled tints the rocky coasts abound,
> And a sad splendour vainly shines around.

It is hard to say if this scene is more "real," or more truly representative of eighteenth-century rural England, than Gray's "Elegy" or Goldsmith's "Deserted Village." One may be inclined to think so because of its insistent grimness, but that is not itself a guarantee of accuracy.

Crabbe's indignation at any rate gives him energy, and this is a good example of strong late Augustan verse. The little allegories that abound in that verse are here—weeds reign despite art and care, thistles threaten war on infants—but the nouns are vibrant because the scene has been carefully observed. Thistles, poppies, bugloss, mallow, and charlock mock, paint, wave, and cling, terrible and alive in their conquest of the sterile soil and the withered stalks of corn. The landscape, completely generalized, has the strength of a Pope portrait. This gives the last couplet above, where Crabbe pulls back from his stubborn observing, a special force. He speaks as if he were a visiting land-scape painter, or a pastoral poet down from London; from the outsider's viewpoint the triumphs of the weeds become "min-gled tints" and "sad splendour" because this perspective can yield no more.

Having created his dreary landscape and drawn a few dreary figures to fit in it, Crabbe has done most of the generalizing about rural poverty he had it in him to do. He knew the parish workhouse at first hand, as the following shows, yet that inti-mate knowledge soon exhausts itself and points nowhere:

> There children dwell who know no parents' care;
> Parents, who know no children's love, dwell there,
> Heartbroken matrons on their joyless bed,
> Forsaken wives, and mothers never wed;
> Dejected widows with unheeded tears,
> And crippled age with more than childhood fears;
> The lame, the blind, and, far the happiest they!
> The gaping idiot and the madman gay.

Of the eight lines here, only "And crippled age with more than childhood fears" does more than give each poorhouse resident a ready-made label. Crabbe's stance is decidedly that of an ob-server, one more person who has come, looked, and left the dejected widow shedding her tears unheeded. In this poem, as in Crabbe's later and better poems, his subject is a real place and the lives people actually led there. But here he gives us gener-alized scenes and emblematic people—heartbroken matrons, wives, and mothers of the workhouse. He had it in him to tell us more about places and the people who live in them than he does here or could do if he continued to write this kind of verse. His temperament guaranteed that he would be primarily an on-looker, but in "The Village" what also gets in his way is that his target really is other writers who have sentimentalized the rural scene. That is why it is a pity that "The Village" has come to be one of the few poems by which Crabbe is known.

After he went more than twenty years without a publication, Crabbe published *The Parish Register* in 1807, followed by *The Borough* and *Tales in Verse.* Since these volumes contain forty thousand lines of verse, it is hard to imagine his writing nothing for two decades and then producing so much very quickly. Yet each book is better than the one preceding, which suggests that Crabbe had to write each one and see it published before he could decide what to do next. Gradually the generalizing habit, which in Crabbe tends to be a preachy habit, gives way to writing that is less emblematic and more narrative, more about individual people who are interesting for their own sake. He continued to write in heroic couplets, but he found a verse that was responsive to people in their environment in ways that his masters, Dryden and Pope, never showed him. Perhaps the fact that he did continue to write heroic couplets is the main reason he has been shunted aside. In his major volumes he is only technically maintaining a tradition; he is writing a poetry that is neither strikingly original nor ever seen before.

Crabbe is usually associated with Aldeburgh. Earlier I said that it was for him primarily a place to leave, but as often happens, leaving is as leaving does. During all his productive years Crabbe lived in parts of eastern England—the Vale of Belvoir was "away," but never so far as to make return difficult or unlikely—but he returned to Aldeburgh much less often than he did to his wife's family's home in Framlingham, some twenty miles inland. Yet Aldeburgh remained the mold into which Crabbe put his materials no matter where he first found them. The town is splendidly described in the opening of *The Borough*, and in another letter in that volume he catalogues its inns and pubs, but he never set out to tell stories that happened only to Aldeburgh people. The widow Goe, Isaac Ashford, Andrew Collett, Robin Dingley, Sir Denys Brand, Blaney, and Clelia, are all put into Crabbe's poetic Borough, but they were based on people and stories that he learned elsewhere and imported into it. Some of these characters live lives of pretense and splendor that few if any could lay claim to in the actual village, and in the poems Crabbe moves up and down the social scale in a way he could not have done in Aldeburgh even had he remained, even had such a wide social spectrum existed there. A foreground / background problem thus arises in both *The Parish Register* and *The Borough*, where the descriptions of the place as a whole would

17

not seem to allow for, or even accommodate, some of the people whose tales are told in detail. We are still a long way from the kind of coherence of people, place, and relative scale that we find in later collections of stories about a single place, like Faulkner's Yoknapatawpha, or even Trollope's Barsetshire. Yet Crabbe knew he was not writing collections of tales of the sort Boccaccio and Chaucer had done. What he had was knowledge of rural, village, and town life that he could claim others did not have; more than that, he seems to have felt, he did not need. If he never conceived of the parish, or the borough, or even the region, as a single place, he did manage to create a variety of ways in which people occupy space, live in restricted areas, and conceive their surroundings. These ways are bound together by little more than their general unlikeness to earlier ways of putting people in places.

We can start with "The Lover's Journey," which offers a representative view of Crabbe's that is also, we can be sure, a corrective to other views then current. Young John goes to visit his beloved Susan, and, being a lover, he calls himself Orlando and calls Susan Laura. Filled with rapturous expectations on his journey, he sees what Crabbe assures us are quite dull scenes and transforms them into beautiful ones in his imagination. He arrives at his destination and discovers that Susan/Laura is not there; so he now dejectedly rides home, through a countryside of rich farm and pastureland, and complains, "There's nothing seen / In this vile country but eternal green." At the outset of the tale, Crabbe quotes Shakespeare on the lunatic, the lover, and the poet, and comments, "It is the soul that sees." The point about John's soul is neatly told, but it seems both simple and labored: Crabbe having a bit of fun. Coleridge's aeolian harps and Wordsworth's musings on the way we "half perceive and half create" could be the targets of "The Lover's Journey," which comes from *Tales in Verse* (1812), but some coarse sentimental fiction is as likely. Crabbe has been so little praised that it seems a shame for F. R. Leavis to have wasted some of that little by claiming that in this poem, "in the use of description, of nature, and the environment generally, for emotional purposes," Crabbe "surpasses any Romantic." Even if one presumes that Leavis

18

was in full agreement with Crabbe's formal view, it is still hard to imagine how he could think "The Lover's Journey" belongs on the same street as "Dejection" or Wordsworth's spots of time.

One reason, though, that Crabbe is much more interesting than his views, and one reason for his great variety of people in places, is that at his best he is always adjusting circumstance, character, and place, getting scale right, and seeking tone and meaning by means of his adjusting. Thus "Peter Grimes," Crabbe's best-known tale, does make a really powerful "use of description, of nature, and the environment generally, for emotional purposes," but Crabbe lets that happen, as it were, as and when he needs it. At the outset of the poem, when young Peter Grimes is protesting his father's Bible reading, calling it "the tyranny of age" against which he seeks to "prove his freedom and assert the man," we have no sense that this is happening in a particular place, or that Crabbe is asking us to understand, in the impotence of Peter's rage, anything about the restricted circumstances of human lots in a fishing town like his borough. Later, in a London workhouse, Peter meets three apprentices. He takes them to his home town and subsequently beats and kills them. All that action also seems to take place on a bare stage. Afterwards the mayor of the borough announces that Grimes must "Hire thee a freeman, whom thou durst not beat," and Peter leaves town; at last he finds "his place," and Crabbe is suddenly absorbed in enveloping him in it, the tide marshes on the edge of town:

> Thus by himself compell'd to live each day,
> To wait for certain hours the tide's delay;
> At the same times the same dull views to see,
> The bounding marsh-bank and the blighted tree;
> The water only, when the tides were high,
> When low, the mud half-covered and half dry;
> The sun-burnt tar that blisters on the planks,
> And bank-side stakes in their uneven ranks;
> Heaps of entangled weeds that slowly float,
> As the tide rolls by the impeded boat.

"Thus by himself compelled to live each day" admits of two

meanings: "By the mayor's order Grimes was compelled to live by himself" and "He was self-compelled to live alone." As we begin the passage, I think we are inclined to read it the first way, Grimes as exile; as the passage moves along, the second way begins to dominate, Grimes compelled "by himself" to come to this ghastly scene, day after day.

Crabbe's placing of Grimes might seem like another emblematic scene. But the effect of having the emphasis move from Grimes as exile to Grimes as self-compelled is to make us see that the scene is, really, just there, on the tidal Alde just south of Aldeburgh. Anyone could go there in a few minutes' walk, but Grimes goes because no one else would—the place is ghastly—and after a while *he* must create it as an emblem:

> When tides were neap, and, in the sultry day,
> Through the tall bounding mud-banks made their way,
> Which on each side rose swelling, and below
> The dark warm flood ran silently and slow;
> There hang his head, and view the lazy tide
> In its hot slimy channel slowly glide;
> Where the small eels that left the deeper way
> For the warm shore, within the shallows play;
> Where gaping mussels, left upon the mud,
> Slope their slow passage to the fallen flood;—
> Here dull and hopeless he'd lie down and trace
> How sidelong crabs had scrawl'd their crooked race;
> Or sadly listen to the timeless cry
> Of fishing gull or clanging golden-eye . . .
> Where all, presented to the eye or ear,
> Oppress'd the soul with misery, grief, and fear.

Crabbe oppresses Grimes's soul with a scene that might well oppress anyone's. He matches landscape to person and makes Grimes the criminal feel only as any innocent reader might feel if faced with these tides and mud-banks. Yet we are also aware that the water, the eels, mussels, and crabs are all just being themselves—which is what we are never asked to feel in Jonson's Penshurst—doing what Crabbe carefully observes them to do. From this double perspective we acknowledge that Grimes, and

20

perhaps the innocent reader as well, wants the landscape to be ghastly or responsive in a way that it really is not. When Grimes then "sees" three spots on the river that mark for him the three lads he has slain, Crabbe has so inveigled us into the scene that it becomes difficult to distinguish between these spots as emanations from a horrid place that anyone might see there and spots that we, innocent readers, can recognize as Grimes's projections of his own guilt. John in "The Lover's Journey," like Shakespeare's lunatics, lovers, and poets, can turn real bushes into imagined bears. Peter's "misery, grief, and fear" are the result of a scene chosen and a scene that oppresses. Crabbe's art is strictly grim, straightforward realism. In the employment of such realism to describe psychological states Crabbe had at least Richardson as his predecessor, but in its use to render the relation of person to place, I'm not sure he had any.

Grimes, terrified by the hypnotic spell the river and his guilt have cast over him, flees back to town.

> A change of scene to him brought no relief;
> In town, 'twas plain, men took him for a thief:
> The sailors' wives would stop him in the street,
> And say, "Now Peter, thou'st no boy to beat":
> Infants at play, when they perceived him, ran,
> Warning each other—"That's the wicked man":
> He growl'd an oath, and in an angry tone
> Cursed the whole place, and wish'd to be alone.

Though the townspeople live only a short distance from Grimes's spot on the river, they know little of its reaches and therefore of Grimes. He is no thief, he is no longer a beater of boys, or, indeed, wicked. Their charges fall from him, not so much untrue as irrelevant, a clatter from which Grimes must escape, though he has no "home" but his crawling muddy riverbank.

We next see him as one of the people of the town might, looking from a distance:

> Fisher he seem'd, yet used no net nor hook;
> Of sea-fowl swimming by no heed he took,

21

But on the gliding waves still fix'd his lazy look:
At certain stations he would view the stream,
As if he stood bewildered in a dream.

Crabbe seems to pull back here, asking us to be onlookers because there is nothing more we can be until something happens
to break the spell. Some people approach Grimes, and ask:
"Wretch, dost thou repent?" He is terrified, not so much of the
questioners as of the question, and so he flees. He is caught,
brought to a parish-bed, and there, shaking with horror, he offers
his testimony and confession.

At the beginning of the tale, we were told about Peter and his
father, but even if we go back and look at them again, they retain
an unrooted inexplicableness. When Grimes confesses, we can
understand why Crabbe had been thus obscure:

"'Twas one hot noon, all silent, still, serene,
No living being had I lately seen;
I paddled up and down and dipp'd my net,
But (such his pleasure) I could nothing get,—
A father's pleasure, when his toil was done,
To plague and torture thus an only son!
And so I sat and look'd upon the stream,
How it ran on, and felt as in a dream:
But dream it was not; no! I fixt my eyes
On the mid stream and saw the spirits rise;
I saw my father on the water stand,
And hold a thin pale boy in either hand;
And there they glided ghastly on the top
Of the salt flood, and never touched a drop;
I would have struck them, but they knew th'intent,
And smiled upon the oar, and down they went."

There is an intentness, a rivetedness on a place, that is new to
literature; Crabbe has sited his action here, on this river, in such
a way that we know it could not have happened anywhere else.

Crabbe is a stern rationalist, and everything in Grimes's
confession has a sternly rational explanation. Grimes turned
away from his father years earlier and now the ghostly figure

returns, mutely accusing Peter of the murder of the three lads, two of whom the father holds aloft. But as Grimes describes his guilt, it is unclear for what crimes, or when; the only thing that is clear is *where* it happened. The moment he is describing must be recent, the father summoned as accuser of his son for the murder of the three boys, but there is also a haunting sense of the accusing father leading his son *toward* these murders, years ago. In any event, the dead children are always versions of Grimes himself. "And so I sat and looked upon the stream"— Grimes does this all his life, madly haunted by guilt and punishment, and in this place.

Crabbe had made no attempt to write of a riveted relation between person and scene before, and, perhaps more surprisingly, he never did so again, never attempted anything like it, though he did go on to explore many other relations of people and places. I want to say, though I have no external supporting evidence, that this place on the tidal Alde, no more than a mile or two from his birthplace, was special for Crabbe, a personal, demanding place. We know of many such places in literature after this, but none before it. Though as a matter of geography Crabbe may have moved only a few miles from the unweeded field of *The Village*, literarily he has moved light years away, from place as idea and emblem to a place and a story that are so local, so linked with events that could only happen here, as to smash our previous glimpses of circumscribed places.

In his opera *Peter Grimes* Benjamin Britten offers an odd, indirect confirmation of my sense that Crabbe could create his haunted Grimes on the river because he himself had been haunted there. Britten was born in Lowestoft, a few miles up the coast from Aldeburgh, and spent much more of his life along this Suffolk coast than Crabbe had done. The Britten music festivals take place annually at Snape, a village on the Alde only a little upstream from Grimes's place on the stream. In making his opera Britten cut out the father, the river, the specters rising in accusation, the capture, and the confession, and he imported pieces from other parts of *The Borough*, most notably the description of the fishers and their families facing a winter storm.

Britten's Peter Grimes is the Outsider, pitted against the villagers as both are set against the elemental force of the sea. All the psychological subtlety of Crabbe's poem is gone, but Britten gains a grim Romantic "use of description, of nature, and the environment generally, for emotional purposes."

Especially given Britten's intimate knowledge of the area, it is hard to believe he did not know what he was doing when he cut the heart out of Crabbe's tale. It is as though—and here I will not apologize for such a phrase of supposing—Britten knew Crabbe had struck a personal nerve with his scenes on the river, and knew someone else should not attempt to touch them. He had that much respect for, and fear of, his predecessor. Of course he had his own medium, his own intentions, his own powerfully and more impersonally conceived place, his own twentieth-century sense of place that seems more like something derived from Emily Brontë or Hardy than from George Crabbe. Still, in his taking on Grimes's story and then not using Crabbe's central scene and feeling, Britten seems to acknowledge that here Crabbe had created a place of personal importance that he should not intrude upon.

I have spent this long with "Peter Grimes" because it seems so personally signed as well as being very good indeed, but it is not indicative of Crabbe's most frequent or characteristic ways of rendering people in places. As I noted earlier, in moving from *The Parish Register* to *The Borough* and then to *Tales in Verse,* Crabbe becomes less emblematic and less preachy; Wordsworth, mindful of Crabbe's popularity at a time when he himself was still relatively obscure, complained that Crabbe only made lists in rhyme. That is not true, but anyone reading Crabbe in bulk knows how garrulous he can be. Perhaps realizing this himself, Crabbe offers much less in the way of chattering journalism in *The Borough* than in *The Parish Register* and much less still in *Tales in Verse.* In the last volume Crabbe drops all pretense that he is writing about a single place or that his tales all come from a single geographical source, and since the pretense did tend to release the merely talky in Crabbe, it was probably just as well.

In *Tales in Verse* Crabbe creates in each story what he calls a "small society." In a preface he explains why he did not attempt to unify his characters into a single "Heroic Poem," or, what would have been more likely, a novel in verse:

> But if these characters which seemed to be at my disposal were not such as would coalesce into one body, nor were of a nature to be commanded by one mind, so neither on examination did they appear as an unconnected multitude, accidentally collected, to be suddenly dispersed; but rather beings of whom might be formed groups and smaller societies . . .

For "unconnected multitude, accidentally collected, to be suddenly dispersed," we may read *The Canterbury Tales* and the *Decameron*, though we might just as easily read *The Parish Register* and *The Borough*. In *Tales in Verse* we have something different, tales drawn on the same scale, "groups and smaller societies," the scale of the local, and in that respect his volume has the kind of unity we can find in Mary Mitford's *Our Village* or Gilbert White's *Natural History of Selborne*.

For Crabbe smallness of scale, social and geographical restriction, were never matters for rejoicing, and in *Tales in Verse* they do not lead to sociological reflection because Crabbe had outgrown his need to insist that he knew much more than others about village and country life. What he gains in this volume is the ability to see the relation of individual choices to restricted circumstance; when he looks at one person making a life, he shows how and to what extent that life was made for that person by place, by circumstance. The range of character and event in the whole volume is quite large, but within each story the range is designedly restricted. I want to show this by looking at two stories, "Arabella" and "The Widow's Tale." Seen from some distance the two seem quite similar and yet, seen close up, each becomes distinctly itself and distinctly revealing of the way Crabbe makes story out of place. Both stories are about women whose education sets them awkwardly apart from others around them, and both women end up marrying men they would have scorned earlier in their lives. If the tales had morals, they would point out the way the passage of time frustrates the ambitions of women who seek to change their lot through education. Fortunately, by this point in his career Crabbe was too absorbed in his individual instances to draw morals.

Arabella's attainments are considerable and widely admired. The "fair town" she lives in is large enough to have in it a whole group of young women, among whom she stands out:

> To every mother were her virtues known,
> And to their daughters as a pattern shown.

Crabbe gives us an indication of the size and the make-up of his small society:

> This reasoning maid, above her Sex's dread,
> Had dared to read, and dared to say she read;
> Not the last novel, not the new-born play;
> Not the mere trash and scandal of the day;
> But (though her young companions felt the shock)
> She studied Berkeley, Bacon, Hobbes, and Locke.

This is a considerable attainment, but at the beginning of the tale Crabbe is not so much interested in Arabella's story, or in taking a line on a young woman reading philosophy, as in showing her effect on her group. She becomes "the wonder of the town" and soon "A thousand eyes were fix'd upon the place," eyes of men come to woo her and of envious women waiting for her to fall. "A thousand eyes" is hardly a precise expression, and "the place" can be Arabella's home or her town, but we understand that her suitors do not come, like Portia's to Belmont, from the world over, yet it is no Aldeburgh she lives in either. A provincial city seems to be Arabella's home, an Ipswich or a Norwich.

Arabella is known as a bluestocking, but Crabbe makes clear she is not against men and is not above being courted. She accepts one suitor but asks him to wait. While he waits he seduces another woman, and Arabella sends him off. Gradually the women who once envied her themselves marry, and she finds that her one remaining friend is another bluestocking, a woman who is proud of being single and lauds her for having turned all her suitors away. Crabbe himself is not scornful of Arabella, or of her mind and its aspirations, but he clearly suspects that his heroine's world, quite large but still circumscribed, does not have in it a man who can match her demands and ideals. Her place is defined by that fact more than it is by any description of her surroundings, because that fact is important and the surroundings are immaterial. Arabella cannot leave her place, and therefore she must either become like her "virgin friend" or else lower her sights; she must not expect a visiting Darcy or a returning Captain Wentworth, and Crabbe does not think it unfair to deny her that expectation. We measure the size and limits of our places by seeing what people and events can be found in them; Crabbe is not so much for or against Arabella as he is absorbed in discovering what she *can* expect.

She can certainly expect time to pass, and Crabbe judiciously informs us that time "varies notions" and "alters hearts." Therefore,

> Let us proceed: twelve brilliant years were past,
> Yet each with less of glory than the last.

Place dictates story. In a much smaller world Arabella might grow angry with that smallness, or we might scorn her for asking the place to give what it almost certainly cannot yield. A much larger world would include travel, London, holiday places. Crabbe gains his even-handed tone by knowing what size his place is, and how little need there is to scorn or pity Arabella. After twelve years of diminishing glory for her, Arabella's world is still large enough to contain suitors, but now it is "only" a merchant who calls, a man she would have quickly rejected earlier.

Arabella does not dismiss the merchant, and her virgin friend, much alarmed, goes in search of something to hold against him and uncovers plenty: he has been abroad and has returned with a woman, an ex-slave apparently, accompanied by their mulatto children—if Arabella wants proof, she can go see them on the green. Arabella is not desperate to marry the man, though she is willing, but before she can accept him she must pay homage to her past aspirations by deceiving herself in the present. If "his heart is evil," she tells herself, "My duty bids me try that heart

27

to mend," a notion of duty whereby she could have married almost anyone years earlier. The effect is wry but not unpleasant, partly because we keep expecting Crabbe to level against Arabella for her reading and her refusal of many decent suitors. Instead, he shows us how we can adapt who we are to where we are. (For a stronger inveighing against those who miss possibilities, he offers "Procrastination" in the same volume.)

From the outset of "The Widow's Tale" we are in a smaller world than Arabella's. Nancy returns from school to the coarse household of her farmer father and brothers—no mother is ever mentioned—and she is forced to see, smell, and even taste the domestic equivalent of Peter Grimes's marshy river. We are not told, but we presume, that Nancy grew up in this house, but having been away she faces it on her return with the shock of discovery:

> When one huge wooden bowl before them stood,
> Fill'd with huge balls of farinaceous food;
> With bacon, mass saline, where never lean
> Beneath the brown and bristly rind was seen;
> When from a single horn the party drew
> Their copious draughts of heavy ale and new;
> When the coarse cloth she saw, with many a stain,
> Soil'd by huge hinds that cut and came again.

If that circumscribes Nancy's world, it is a small one indeed, but worlds this small exist and neither she nor we can know if she is doomed to remain there. Nancy does hope enough, though, to reject a coarse young farmer, Henry Carr, when he comes courting: "A slave! a drudge! she could not, for her life!"

For her life, forever? Arabella has major attainments, Nancy has only been away to school. Nancy's disgust at a family content with bacon fat and huge beer jugs is quite different from Arabella's considered declining of apparently eligible suitors. Their worlds are different, to be sure, but to read a number of the *Tales in Verse* consecutively is to see how little Crabbe has to adjust his position, or scope, to alter place and its possibilities.

Nancy's world is smaller than Arabella's, to say nothing of being less refined, less well educated, and less clean; Nancy must therefore tolerate more and realize that Henry Carr is not just one in a string of suitors. Yet Nancy's world is large enough to have some class distinctions besides "school" and "huge balls of farinaceous food"; one of Nancy's coarse brothers points them out to her:

"Here," said the Brother, "are no ladies seen—
That is a widow dwelling on the green;
A dainty dame, who can but barely live
On her poor pittance, yet contrives to give;
She happier days has known, but seems at ease,
And you may call her lady, if you please:
But if you wish, good sister, to improve,
You shall see twenty better worth your love."

It is a packed and impressive speech. Crabbe is so careful in the creation of his places that on the basis of the brother's speech we should be able to guess with reasonable accuracy how large this village is and what Nancy's prospects are. There are no ladies in this village, the brother says, though Nancy is free to call this "dainty dame" a lady if she likes. He seems to equate "lady" with a certain income, which this widow clearly does not have; and if Nancy wants to improve herself, why there are "twenty better worth your love." "Twenty" seems a term like "a thousand eyes" in "Arabella," and so the population of the village need not be more than a few hundred. In such a setting Nancy can expect more suitors perhaps, but not many who are different from Henry Carr. But our attention is now on the widow.

Her table is not dominated by a huge wooden bowl, and her cloth is not hacked and stained; she reads, she grows flowers in her garden. Nancy must idealize her, and the widow, realizing this, must disabuse her. Her garden, she says, "tempts not a feeble dame who dreads the cold," and "books are soon painful for my failing sight." She then tells Nancy the story of her life, and it is perfect for showing the young woman her possibilities and limits. She once rejected many lovers and finally accepted a penniless assistant in her father's office. After years of being too poor to marry, the assistant undertook a voyage to make money, but ship and fiancé both sank. Nancy is quick to ask how the woman became a widow. Her world, it turned out, was large enough to contain another suitor; she married him, and he was a good man and it was a good marriage. Except, alas, she could not give him her heart, a fact one cannot predict and one that no world is too small or too large to contain, for it can happen anywhere:

> "Alas! of every early hope bereft
> There was no fondness in my bosom left."

Nancy's world, she can see even without the widow's pointing it out, is so small that she had better take the widow's tale as a talisman of her own. Dreading *"their* fate / Who plan too wildly, and are wise too late,"* Nancy returns home and agrees to marry Henry Carr.

If one thinks back no earlier than a generation before Crabbe's, to Fielding's inset stories of Mr. Wilson and the Man on the Hill, or to those in Johnson's *Rasselas,* one can see how different "The Widow's Tale" is from them. In various ways Fielding's and Johnson's tales seek large exemplifying status—thus I spent my youth, and this is what happened to me, and from this you can learn what all who thus spend their youth can expect. Crabbe hugs a nearer shore: my possibilities were created by where I was, and as I discovered the limits of those possibilities, I discovered my place and my life. The widow's tale has clear meaning for Nancy only because both live in the same place; put them in the world of "Arabella," to say nothing of Portia's Belmont, and it would all have been different; why, Portia's Belmont can even include in it Shylock's daughter.

Many have been put off by Crabbe because his being so little a partisan, an enthusiast, or a supporter of causes seemed a sure sign that he was indifferent to the lots of those whose tales he told. My sense of him is that he is an original inventor of place as outlining story and human possibility, but this cannot satisfy readers who are outraged that Crabbe never asked life to be different from the way he found it. He can be unnerving, no question, especially in his very best stories. But, to come back for a last look at "The Widow's Tale," he does not gloat that Nancy ends up agreeing to marry Henry Carr. Indeed, in an especially nice touch, he gives the last word to Nancy's father; it is for him to eulogize the widow, and in terms that reveal just how large this village—and, by extension, Nancy's possibilities—is, and are:

> "Oft have I smiled, when I beheld her pass
> With cautious step, as if she hurt the grass;
> Where if a snail's retreat she chanced to storm,
> She look'd as if begging pardon of the worm;
> And what, said I, still laughing at the view,
> Have these weak creatures in the world to do?
> But some are made for action, some to speak;
> And while she looks so pitiful and meek,
> Her words are weighty, though her nerves are weak."

It is not by itself a speech that creates any sense of place at all, but coming near the end it illuminates a tale of human impulses reaching out and having their surrounding place shape them.

The rough farmer of the huge bowl, dreadful food, and limited outlook has lived for years not far from the widow, whose roses and books belie her currently sad life. He has known her only as a timid soul afraid to disturb the pathway of a snail, and, incurious soul that he is, had Nancy never recoiled from home on her return from school, he would never have known the widow except as a fixed figure in the landscape. But the widow helped shape Nancy's life, and that is how she comes out of the landscape and into Nancy's father's life, and for that the farmer clumsily expresses his gratitude. Crabbe moves so easily around his village in this tale that we may not notice him doing so, as he quietly realizes his effects.

In 1812, the year "The Widow's Tale" was given to the public, Jane Austen, then thirty-seven, wrote in a busy letter to her sister: "Miss Lee I found very conversible; she admires Crabbe as she ought. She is at an age of reason, ten years older than myself at least." Austen moved in large spaces, despite her reputation for living and working restrictedly. She meets a Miss Lee and in a few minutes finds out more about her than Nancy's father found out about the widow in years of living as her near neighbor. Yet though Austen is thus practically a citizen of the world, if not a companion to Beau Brummel or Caroline Lamb, she had known and long admired the poems of Crabbe, "as she ought." Austen knew about restricted space, to be sure, but at age thirty-seven she was still full of romance, and was about to wish into being some romantic possibilities that she knew Crabbe and Miss Lee and others who had reached the age of reason would find extremely unlikely. To wit: the mousy cousin from Portsmouth comes to Northamptonshire and marries the spiritual heir to a great estate, in the process becoming that estate's real heir herself; the spoiled and wealthy princess in a Surrey village finally learns that the prince is not the frog but the gentleman next door she has always treated like her father; the girl who throws away her best chances at age nineteen discovers at age twenty-seven that she has all these chances again and more. Crabbe left no recorded opinion of Austen's novels, but he may have admired them without believing in their assessments of actual possibilities. By the time he wrote his best poems he had, by Austen's calculations, reached the age of reason; more important, he had lived in spaces more enclosed than Austen's and saw fewer possibilities for his Nancy, his widow, his Arabella even, than Austen wished for her later heroines. Perhaps East Anglia had less scope than did the Home Counties. In any event, Austen would assent to Crabbe's premise about real, specific spaces doing much to shape destinies; this notion would have baffled anyone from Ben Jonson to Samuel Johnson.

"And some day," writes Ezra Pound, "when Arthur's tomb is no longer an object for metrical research, and when the Albert Memorial is no longer regilded, Crabbe's people will still remain vivid. People will read Miss Austen because of her knowledge of the human heart, and not solely for her refinement." If one is comparing Crabbe and Austen with, say, Wordsworth or Dickens, one easily thinks of his vividness and her knowledge of the human heart as belonging to the eighteenth century, the end of the Augustan tradition. In that tradition, in Leavis' words, "what seemed most significant to individual experience was not discrepant with the claim of the common sense world to be the pre-eminently and authoritatively real." But Crabbe's way of being Augustan, which in these terms he certainly is, also makes him an important figure in the great generations of change. Crabbe's language is much less memorable, much less metaphorical than Pope's or even Johnson's, because the circumstances of his characters, when considered by the claim of common sense, neither demanded nor needed more. Likewise, when place helps dictate story, it creates a literature which must be seen as a provincializing of the Augustan tradition, a diminishing of its possibilities. Crabbe's characters thus achieve less and yield less in the way of generalization than do Flecknoe and David, Belinda or Atticus, and about his people their maker has only home truths to offer: dreams fade, time passes, poverty hurts, profligacy gorges itself, the meanest fidelity and loyalty must be honored. In his transitional age the nature of generalization begins to alter, because people are no longer emblems but individuals, and what happens to one does not make a pattern for another.

There would come a time when it could be said that all lives are provincial, but Crabbe did not live in that time either. Compared to the great provincials like Cathy and Heathcliff, Maggie Tulliver, Tess, Jude, or Paul Morel, Crabbe's characters, little figures in stories tending to run no more than five hundred lines, seem almost like marionettes for all their vividness, and Crabbe seems more an observer than someone actively engaged in life itself. His people do not say or do the powerful and decisive thing. In these novels place works its will on a child, and the result is scenes so rooted and powerful as to make Crabbe's tales seem positively normative, generalized, Augustan, "Peter Grimes" excepted. But these are historical statements, not judgments of relative merit. Crabbe's reputation has suffered because these two have been confused, because it is difficult historically to place him in his own time.

Knowing his limits, Crabbe restricted himself to tales, and then turned that limitation into strength. In one story a man drinks and becomes a brute, in another a man drinks and he and his little world are happier thereby. In one story a young couple do not seize the day and eventually part; in another they do marry young but the man then abandons his mate; in a third, the couple are prudent and end up living happily. Always, it takes only slight adjustments in character and place to make all the difference, and because he knew so well the little things that end up mattering, Crabbe's people will remain vivid when Arthur's tomb is no longer an object for metrical research. He worked with shrewdness, intelligence, dignity, and insight, always seeming to stand on the other, the older side of the edge of change, but actually walking in uncharted terrain.

# III

### ❧ JANE AUSTEN

JANE AUSTEN liked to get her details right. She used a calendar to date the weeks and months in her novels. She calculated, and then openly stated, the income and financial expectations of her characters. She knew how far it was from one place to another, and how long a journey it was. If she did not have to go see Northamptonshire in order to set *Mansfield Park* there, she needed to know if it "is a county of hedgerows." (We must presume, incidentally, that she was told it was not; shrubbery and an iron gate are the significant details of landscape in *Mansfield Park* and the hedgerow scene came later, in the Somerset of *Persuasion*.)

One marvel of her fiction is the way her precision is employed; Austen can take bits and pieces of geography and landscape and transform them into social tone and moral suggestion in a sentence or two. Journeys are a case in point. No trip is of major importance in any of the novels, but Austen can use a journey to convey a great deal very quickly. When Elinor Dashwood in *Sense and Sensibility* learns that Willoughby left London for Somerset that morning and stopped only for ten minutes in Marlborough, she begins to relent and consents to hear his confession; the man may be corruption itself, but passionate feeling can be measured by how far and fast he has come. Elizabeth Bennet in *Pride and Prejudice* walks the three miles between Longbourn and Netherfield to see her sick sister Jane and does not worry about getting her boots wet or her clothes muddy, and she thereby sets herself apart from everyone else in the novel; good health and strong loving concern mark a heroine here, and it comes as no surprise to learn that Elizabeth is not much of a reader. Frank Churchill in *Emma* does *not* go from Highbury to London, a matter of fourteen miles, just to get a haircut, but his pretext illustrates his foppishness, his advertised willingness to make such a journey for such a purpose. William Price goes from Mansfield Park to Portsmouth and back by way of London, whereas Fanny goes by way of Oxford. Nothing is said about the matter, but Austen has found a way to tell us that she is keeping Fanny away from London and the corrupting taint of the Crawfords, the Frasers, and Wimpole Street.

Each journey gains its tone from the book it is in; so too with her places. Ever since Austen wrote her niece that "3 or 4 families in a Country Village is the very thing to work on," it has too frequently been assumed she is describing her own practice as well as giving advice. When Mary Mitford writes that "nothing is so delightful as to sit down in one of Miss Austen's novels, quite sure before we leave it to become intimate with every spot and every person it contains," she really can only be describing *Emma*, the only one of the six novels which is about 3 or 4 families in a well described country village. By comparison most places in *Pride and Prejudice* are only faintly described, characters go back and forth between Hertfordshire and Kent without seeming to change their place at all, and they even go via London without getting tainted. Austen changed, her society was changing, and her sense of places and placedness had to change too. There is a great difference between the Bath of *Northanger Abbey* and the Bath of *Persuasion*, between the London of *Sense and Sensibility* and the London of *Mansfield Park*. It is three miles between Longbourn and Netherfield in *Pride and Prejudice*, and three miles between Kellynch and Uppercross in *Persuasion*, but they seem different distances entirely and measure very different things.

Among novelists Austen is, as Marvin Mudrick has claimed, world champion novelist, and yet she has been as difficult to place historically as George Crabbe or John Clare. What she created were tones earlier writers did not need and later writers could not use; she has had no heirs. As a result, writers on the novel, and writers on her period, have in different ways been forced to twist and turn to face her squarely. What is important about her historically, I think, is that she is Wordsworth's contemporary and that they are the two great writers of their time. He trailed more traces of the old culture than she, and for that reason hers is the purer and stronger response to her own time.

Until the moment in *Pride and Prejudice* when Elizabeth and the Gardiners set off to see the Lakes, Austen was content to have *ideas* of place and places, ideas that were commonplace in the years when she was precociously growing up. Catherine Morland has an idea of place, and Henry Tilney, when he corrects hers, can only substitute another idea. Hers is literary Gothic, Northanger Abbey as a place in Mrs. Radcliffe's Italian Alps. It is absurd, and Henry Tilney scorns it:

> "Does our education prepare us for such atrocities? Do our laws connive at them? Could they be perpetuated without being known, in a country like this, where social and literary intercourse is on such a footing; where every man is surrounded by a neighbourhood of voluntary spies, and where roads and newspapers lay everything open?"

The sequence works just like an irony in a Fielding novel, and Catherine's imaginings serve as the cant that Henry's ridicule then exposes. Place is not literary, he claims, and England is ordinary life lived in a Christian island.

But Henry is wrong, and the novel shows that his too is only an idea. He says that everyone in England is "surrounded by a neighbourhood of voluntary spies"; it was just this phrase that D. W. Harding underlined to identify Austen's "regulated hatred." But while undoubtedly Austen herself was thus surrounded and may well have imagined Catherine and Henry in such an environment, *Northanger Abbey* offers no such neighborhood, no network of spies, no sense of people living adjacent to each other. It is one of the novel's best touches that General Tilney, though he is not Montoni and does not lock up his wife, is nonetheless a villain, a tyrant of property, marriage, and inheritance so that England, Christian island or not, knows an evil much like Mrs. Radcliffe's Alps. This point Austen certainly was aware of, but of a related one she may not have been. In order to keep General Tilney misinformed about Catherine's wealth, or lack of it, Austen, having no neighborhood of voluntary spies in the novel, is forced to use John Thorpe as the General's source of information. That the two should know each other is unlikely, because the General does not spend his time whipping horses around the countryside in curricles and Thorpe does little else; that anyone could give credence to anything Thorpe says is preposterous, because he is a swaggering ass, as even Catherine can discover. In other words, Austen may want to convey that Henry Tilney is right and Catherine is wrong about England, but people and places are so feebly understood and described in *Northanger Abbey* that Henry's England is only a landscape of the mind.

Something similar happens in *Sense and Sensibility* in the often-quoted conversation between Marianne Dashwood and Edward Ferrars in which she embraces the picturesque and he insists that only use and usefulness make the land good to look at. One knows how the dialogue came to be written. Marianne is conceived as a late-eighteenth-century young woman of sensibility, one given to speeches that begin "Dear Norland! when shall I cease to regret you!" Part of her emotional equipment, therefore, must be attachment to picturesque landscapes, though she knows that in her time such taste has become "mere jargon." Ferrars must then be given the staunch bucolic Augustan side of the debate in order to show that Austen knows as well as Pope that it is use alone that justifies expense. The trouble is that the novel refuses to be obedient to the lines of force this conversation has seemingly set down. Marianne soon ceases to be the burlesque figure she was at first. She much prefers Willoughby's recitation of poetry to Ferrars', and well she might, for all agree Ferrars mumbles. She favors Willoughby's manners and affectionate disposition, and it makes sense that she should; even Elinor, knowing Willoughby is a careless rake, must finally acknowledge that the happy and affectionate man Marianne fell in love with is as genuine a part of his character as any other. On the other hand, Ferrars' preference for land used purposefully is only an idea that floats unattached in the novel. We do not see land used thus in the book and Ferrars himself is, for the most part, himself useless. So here too place is an idea, stated but unembodied.

It is not at all surprising that *Northanger Abbey* and *Sense and Sensibility* are much the weakest of the six completed novels. As to why this should be so, one reason is not far to seek. Little in Austen's reading could have given her more than ideas of places or landscapes, and in her life she seems for a long time to have assumed her place so implicitly and fully that she felt no need to render places in her fiction or put people in clearly defined places. The novels are set in the southern counties of England, and Austen herself was able to move within this region with unselfconscious ease and a clear sense that this was her world. Most of *Pride and Prejudice* too, though vastly superior in other ways, is not anchored in place. Kent and Hertfordshire are interchangeable, Meryton is any place where soldiers are barracked, and houses are distinguished by the annual income of their owners. Though some of the liveliest dialogue ever written is in this novel, it is spoken on something quite close to a bare stage.

*Pride and Prejudice* was published in 1813, but an earlier form of the novel, *First Impressions*, was finished before the turn of the century. In between came Austen's father's retirement in 1801 from the living at Steventon and the family's subsequent move to Bath; the Reverend Austen died in 1805 and the others then moved to Southampton. As far as anyone can tell, Austen did no writing during these years and her life was unsettled and unhappy. But in 1809 her brother Edward established Austen and her mother in Chawton, Hampshire, and she soon became a published author: *Sense and Sensibility*, also finished years before (1811); *First Impressions* revised into *Pride and Prejudice* (1813); *Mansfield Park* (1814); *Emma* (1816); *Persuasion*, published posthumously after Austen's death in 1817; *Northanger*

*Abbey*, probably written first, published last in 1818. The three early ones are thus Steventon novels, and the three later Chawton novels.

The great scenes at Pemberley in *Pride and Prejudice* are Austen's first important essays of a place. I am fond of supposing that these scenes do not belong to *First Impressions* but to the novel as revised at Chawton, but no evidence exists beyond the fact that these chapters are something Austen never attempted in the other early novels or in the earlier parts of this one. Even before Pemberley, Elizabeth and Darcy have earned their place among the greatest romantic couples in literature, precisely because their conversations are neither romantic nor standard sex war skirmishes. Although the two are verbally guarded, they let themselves be vulnerable, and their talk makes them expressive and implicated at every turn. But it takes Pemberley to make them lovers.

R. W. Chapman calls it "grotesque" to suggest that "Elizabeth was first brought round by the sight of the wealth and grandeur of Pemberley," but only because he states the matter too simply. Elizabeth has known all along that Pemberley must be expensive and grand, and, in one sense, she began to be "brought round" in her first conversation with Darcy. Yet the very unplacedness and uprootedness of those conversations—they take place mostly at Bingley's Netherfield or at Lady Catherine's Rosings, where neither is much at home—have made it difficult for either to extricate self from situation long enough to see how much sex, romance, and intimacy has been engendered by their talks.

It is Elizabeth's seeing Pemberley as a place, Darcy's place, that extricates her:

> They gradually ascended for half a mile, and then found themselves at the top of a considerable eminence, where the wood ceased, and the eye was instantly caught by Pemberley House, situated on the opposite side of a valley, into which the road with some abruptness wound. It was a large, handsome, stone building, standing well on rising ground, and backed by a ridge of high, woody hills;—and in front, a stream of some natural importance was swelled into greater, but without any artificial appearance. Its banks were neither formal, nor falsely adorned.

Elizabeth was delighted. She had never seen a place for which nature had done more, or where natural beauty had been so little counteracted by an awkward taste. They were all of them warm in their admiration; and at that moment she felt, that to be mistress of Pemberley might be something!

Austen had never been to Derbyshire, and it was a brilliant stroke to place Pemberley there, as though she were saying that the places she did know farther south were too self-consciously the work of landscape architects. Up north, outside her ken, nature could happily be imagined free, the stream remaining itself as it widened, the hills behind remaining wooded, though presumably maintained.

As a description, this is in the tradition of poets like Thomson. If Pemberley itself was not built for envious show, it does offer this eminence to show it off, and, *pace* Edward Ferrars, use here is not what justifies expense. Yet its appeal is not an aesthetic feast for the eye so much as it is an expression of its owner. Without being in any worked-out way symbolic, wood, stream, hill, and house here are all Darcy; the whole may seem remote and aloof, but Elizabeth can sense it is not so really, though it is indeed proud. It is a mistake to conclude that Elizabeth thinks it would be "something" to be Pemberley's mistress as a matter of ownership; obviously what she is responding to is the estate as the expression of Darcy.

In her conversation with Darcy's housekeeper, in her walk down the stream and into the woods, and especially in her conversations with Darcy himself, Elizabeth becomes clearer about that "something." He is unexpectedly easy, courteous, and generous without calculation, and perhaps for the first time in literature a character looks, feels, and acts differently at home than abroad, in a place that allows for a different, truer self to emerge:

The introduction [of Darcy to the Gardiners], however, was immediately made; and as she named their relationship to herself, she stole a sly glance at him, to see how he bore it; and was not without the expectation of his decamping as fast as he could from such disgraceful companions. That he was *surprised* by the connexion was evident; he sustained it however with fortitude, and so far from going away, turned back with them, and entered into conversation with Mr. Gardiner. Elizabeth could not but be pleased, could not but triumph. It was consoling, that he should know she had some relations for whom there was no need to blush.

Darcy's love of Elizabeth, the Gardiners' excellence, and Elizabeth's pride in their excellence, all can flower in this particular landscape; it permits wealthy landowner, gentleman's daughter, and relations in trade to be all equally admiring, equally at ease.

The three Pemberley chapters take up much less space in the novel than they do in memory, and they mark where place begins to assume an important role in Austen's handling of her actions. If, as in my supposing, they were the result of her settling at Chawton, it is plain to see how the years in Bath and Southampton could give her a need for a home where she could be herself more easily than elsewhere; after Pemberley, none of her central characters is easily "at home" in the southern counties. In *Mansfield Park* and *Emma*, which were to follow hard on the heels of the publication of *Pride and Prejudice*, place assumes a major role in Austen's imagination; everyone has a place, and a tone that derives from a place, and people thrive or droop, depending on where they are. Wonderful as they are, the Pemberley chapters are really just a grand concoction compared to the pervasive relation of person to place in the next two novels.

On January 29, 1813, Austen wrote her sister a letter that has never been easy to figure out:

> Now I will try to write of something else, and it shall be a complete change of subject—ordination—I am glad to find your enquiries have ended so well. If you would discover whether Northamptonshire is a county of hedgerows, I should be glad again.

Austen had just received her first copies of *Pride and Prejudice* and, though she implies here she was about to begin *Mansfield Park*, a note that was found after she died says that novel was begun in 1811. There are other complications: Northamptonshire was and is a county of hedgerows, but there is no mention of them in *Mansfield Park*, and Edmund Bertram's ordination is hardly the subject of the novel. Yet Austen was not given to throwing dust in her sister's eyes.

The subject of *Mansfield Park* would seem to be Mansfield Park rather than ordination, and the novel would seem to be placed in Northamptonshire for the same reason Pemberley is in Derbyshire, namely, it lies sufficiently removed from Austen's knowledge for her to imagine her place freely. In his famous essay about the novel, Lionel Trilling writes of Mansfield Park as if it were one of the allegorical places in *The Faerie Queene*:

> It shuts out the world and the judgment of the world. The sanctions on which it relies are not those of culture, of quality of being, of personality, but precisely those which the new conception of the moral life minimizes, the sanctions of principle.

By Trilling's reckoning, the novel at the end gets rid of all those who do not adhere to Mansfield's code: Mary and Henry Crawford, the Bertram sisters, the Rushworths, the Grants, and Mrs. Norris. A rather drastic piece of housecleaning but, so the argument goes, a necessary one. I think, however, that Trilling's view distorts the novel, because most of the housecleaning, the shutting out of the world and the judgment of the world, comes in the disastrously simplifying last chapter, the one that begins "Let other pens dwell on guilt and misery," and then proceeds, by dwelling on guilt and misery, to kill the novel off as much as end it. To do better justice to the novel as a whole and at least try to speak to the puzzling sentences in Austen's letter, I will write about *Mansfield Park* as if that chapter were not there, and then consider the consequences of the fact that it is. It is important to stress that this was Austen's first attempt to start a book in something like fifteen years; in many ways she was moving into unknown territory that was not light or bright or sparkling and certainly did not want for shade.

Austen's conception of Mansfield, though quite unlike the allegorical places in *The Faerie Queene*, does not require that it be described visually or geographically. It has a vicarage connected to the estate, Sotherton is seven miles away, and that is almost all we are given. We learn nothing of Sir Thomas Bertram's actions as a landowner, as we do of Darcy's and George Knightley's. We hear of walks along paths, and shrubbery, but have no idea of the extent of the place, or of how much of Sir Thomas' income derives from it and how much from his plantations in Antigua. Mansfield Park's importance as a place emerges slowly as the novel proceeds, but it never demands clear description.

We do hear a great deal about education, more here than in any other Austen novel. R. W. Chapman, apparently seeing the matter as Trilling does, writes: "The ostensible moral of the book, which is almost blatantly didactic, is that education, religious and moral, is omnipotent over character." Chapman does not say what the un-ostensible or subversive moral of the book is, but one might begin to uncover it by saying that, by Chapman's or Trilling's terms of reckoning, Sir Thomas Bertram is close to being a complete failure. In the following passage we have what I think all would agree is typical *Mansfield Park* rhetoric; it comes when Julia Bertram, on the visit to Sotherton, breaks down under the pressure of her sister Maria's malice and Henry Crawford's indifference:

> The politeness which she had been brought up to practice as a duty made it impossible for her to escape; while the want of that higher species of self-command, that just consideration of others, that knowledge of her own heart, that principle of right, *which had not formed any essential part of her education*, made her miserable under it.

This way of writing, solemn and severe, is for long stretches of the novel Austen's way of showing us Mansfield as a place. In none of her other novels would we find the clause I have put in italics; it defines the intellectual and moral weather of this novel and its effect here is to soften the judgment against Julia and to point to her family, especially to her father, as the source of the superficiality of her moral understanding.

Sir Thomas has married Maria Ward, a woman overcome by weakness and weariness, a fit companion or teacher for no one. Her sister is the conniving and toadying Mrs. Norris. It is to these mentors that Sir Thomas entrusts the education of the three girls, and for years he is either blind to or indifferent to the results of that education, though he seldom speaks without saying the results matter greatly to him. When we see the children as adults for the first time, Sir Thomas is off in Antigua (where, we gather, all is not well either) and we see clearly that Julia is weak, Tom is a wastrel, and Maria is worse. The mice hope to play while the cat is away; they take the cue from Tom's friend Yates and plan a performance of *Lovers' Vows*.

Tom, Maria, and Julia see nothing wrong with amateur theatricals, but they know their father would object even if they cannot fathom his reasons. Nor does he really explain himself after he suddenly returns; Yates, though hardly a thoughtful soul, thinks of him as "unintelligibly moral." Then, rather than try to be intelligible, Sir Thomas "could not help giving Mrs. Norris a hint of his having hoped that her advice might have been interposed to prevent what her judgment must certainly have disapproved"—which is quite typical of him, and preposterous. Mrs. Norris never disapproves of the theatricals, she would not necessarily have interposed if she had, and the youngsters would have prevailed in any event. If Sir Thomas cannot see this, it is hard to know what he can see. So too with another concern of his, Maria's engagement. Sir Thomas sees how silly Mr. Rushworth is and realizes that Maria's behavior to him is careless and cold, but having expressed his concern, he is content to play Lear to her Goneril and to say no more after she tells him that "she had the highest esteem for Mr. Rushworth's character and disposition, and could not have a doubt of her happiness with him." Translated, that means she will do anything to get away from Mansfield Park.

Let us imagine that the subject of the book *is* ordination. Two years into the writing of *Mansfield Park* and only six months from completing it, Austen in her letter can hardly be referring to Edmund's ordination as the subject of the novel, because that takes place offstage and makes no difference to Edmund's feelings or conduct. If I say that the church is Mansfield Park, and that the one ordained is Fanny, I am speaking in a way I feel sure Austen would not, though this does seem to be what the novel enacts. Mansfield has doctrines about education and the moral life, and though they may be unspoken everyone assumes them to be there, to be embraced or rejected. In the face of Sir Thomas' spiritual laziness, his absorption in outward signs, the whole task of seeking Mansfield's inward and spiritual grace falls upon Edmund and especially on Fanny. The novel is long because Austen is mainly interested in the process whereby Mansfield comes to be itself or gain its first true owners. It takes, for instance, many years and half the novel for Fanny to change from being frightened to being mistrustful without becoming a mistrustful person; it takes a long time for us to see why that is so important.

Being mistrustful is first learning not to be afraid of everything, and then learning what can be trusted. Edmund releases Fanny from her total fearfulness as a child, and she slowly learns that she seldom can trust anyone other than Edmund, and not always him. Put that way, it is clear how much adjusting of person to place is necessary to make the small scale of the thing seem important and rewarding. Mansfield the place can teach better than its inhabitants. One evening, when the Crawfords are dallying at Mansfield, Fanny steps outside with Edmund to look at the sky, both aware that he will soon be trying to return to be close to Mary:

> "Here's harmony," said she; "here's repose! Here's what may leave all painting and music behind, and that poetry can only attempt to describe! Here's what may tranquilize every care, and lift the heart to rapture! When I look out on such a night as this, I feel as if there could be neither wickedness nor sorrow in the world; and there would be less of both if the sublimity of Nature were more attended to, and people were carried more out of themselves by contemplating such a scene."

As doctrine, this is Shaftesburian-Wordsworthian, solid eighteenth-century stuff. In Fanny it is exclamation, release from being nobody to being passionately tranquil, and with Edmund. Fanny can trust Nature, and trust herself to place Nature rightly in a set of values others may ignore or threaten.

Some time later Fanny comes to another belief dear to Wordsworth, one that is crucial for Fanny, as heir to Mansfield, to take in. She is walking with Mary Crawford at the vicarage, noticing the improvements the Grants have made in their shrubbery and walks. Fanny's speech is quite long and, for her, surprisingly self-assertive, indicating a desire to trust Mary and an increase in her trust in herself:

> "If any one faculty of our nature may be called *more* wonderful than the rest, I do think it is memory. There seems something more speakingly incomprehensible in the powers, the failures, the inequalities of memory, than in any of our other intelligences . . . We are, to be sure, a miracle in every way; but our powers of recollecting and forgetting do seem peculiarly past finding out."

It *is* doctrine, and Fanny's speechifying, whenever we remove it from its immediate context, can make us long for some bright, or snappy, remark of Elizabeth Bennet's or Emma's, but it is important for Austen, as she slowly explores the way Mansfield is a place and Fanny is its heir, that she avoid wit.

Why it is crucial that Fanny know the "speakingly incomprehensible" quality of memory is made clear in the great scene between her and Sir Thomas, after Henry Crawford has proposed to Fanny. She has been creating a habit of trust and belief, and after Henry proposes Fanny remembers how he had behaved at Sotherton, flirting cruelly with Maria. That is how she can, in the face of the proposal, and Edmund's absence, and Sir Thomas' turning on her, save everything: because she trusts her memory. If she accepts Mr. Crawford she will make Sir Thomas happy, she will become important in everyone's eyes, there will be no bar to Edmund's marrying Mary, and, in effect, Mansfield Park's walls will come tumbling down.

What Fanny remembers of Henry makes his current interest in her irrelevant; he may well and truly love her, but that does not matter, and everything in Jane Austen's power has been exerted to make Fanny, humorless mousy Fanny, into a true heroine at this moment:

> "Have you any reason, child, to think ill of Mr. Crawford's temper?"

47

"No, sir."

She longed to add, "but of his principles I have"; but her heart sank under the appalling prospect of discussion, explanation, and probable non-conviction. Her ill opinion of him was chiefly founded on observations, which, for her cousins' sake, she could scarcely dare mention to their father. Maria and Julia, and especially Maria, were so implicated in Mr. Crawford's misconduct, that she could not give his character, such as she believed it, without betraying them. She had hoped that, to a man like her uncle, so discerning, so honourable, so good, the simple acknowledgment of settled *dislike* on her side, would have been sufficient. To her infinite grief she found it was not.

Mansfield *now* is a place of residing value, and Fanny, herself discerning, honorable, and good, embodies it. She cannot trust Sir Thomas to embrace what he claims to value, but she can trust herself to do so.

This is the best example we have seen so far of what can be done when, with the old culture and the generalized landscape gone, the scope of action is reduced to small, restricted, and "real" spaces. The contrast between Fanny and the lovers of *Pride and Prejudice* is striking. Even without their scenes at Pemberley, Elizabeth and Darcy can be put anywhere and they will shine as brightly as any pair of the world's lovers, but prim and frightened Fanny can emerge as a person of consequence only when space has been reduced to a single place. Crabbe learned many secrets of what reduction of scale, and subsequent widening and closing of focus, can achieve, but neither he nor anyone before him attempted anything like what Austen does here in letting Fanny, just by her stubborn silence, save and create Mansfield Park at this moment of crisis.

The scenes in Portsmouth that follow are remarkable for many things, notably for the speed and deftness with which Austen shows us the squalid chaos of the Price household. Because of that, Mansfield is clarified for Fanny as a *place* of value; hitherto she has had little need to say its name, but now she does, over and over. Fanny and Austen both can afford to feel that wealth, comfort, and settledness matter, not because they are crucially important but because their absence is so painful. Mansfield has always been an idea in Austen's mind and gradually it has become one in Fanny's as well, a place of stern rectitude where memory is the only defense against all the temptations and display that urge forgetfulness. In Portsmouth, nostalgia for Mansfield is also a matter of good servants, clean plates, and sufficiently ordered lives; it is clear that possibilities for education and ordination lie *there*, where Fanny has been and where, she can now see, her equally educable sister Susan has not.

At this point Austen's interest in *Mansfield Park* is almost over. It is as if those qualities in Austen that created Elizabeth and Darcy, qualities that celebrate the ability of certain special people to achieve what others cannot and do not deserve, grew impatient with the slow, heavy accumulation of *Mansfield Park*'s concerns. Fanny Price, after all, not Emma Woodhouse, is her heroine that "no one will like." Having arrived at a point where Mansfield has emerged as an embodied idea and a place, Austen found the rest too tedious to work out at the pace she had been employing to arrive at this point. What she offers, to wind up the novel quickly, is Henry Crawford's sudden collapse into the willing arms of Maria Rushworth—in London, where such things happen—and it is possible to believe this of him, or believe in his genuine love for Fanny, but not both. Then there is the chance meeting of Julia and Yates so they can elope and be whisked away. Finally, and worst of all, we have the only love scene between Edmund and Fanny taken up with his account of his final meeting with Mary Crawford, who is now inexplicably willing to collapse into the role of wife to a country parson. Then comes the dreadful last chapter in which Austen passes her characters before us, and blesses or curses them according to proper Mansfield doctrine. Place triumphs, but in a way that might make anyone want to forsake Mansfield, move to London, and take one's best chances. Here all the careful adjusting of person to scale that makes this novel so impressive is abandoned, and I am convinced it is the shock of seeing what Mansfield would look like if it were *not* carefully and painstakingly rendered that has made it seem repellent to many readers, who in effect are reading the tone of the last chapter back into the rest of the novel.

What is needed is only a decent slowness. There is no reason Edmund and Fanny are denied what Austen happily gives her other major lovers, namely scenes in which the discovery of a long-existing and long-denied love flowers into relaxed and triumphant recollection. Mansfield, dedicated to the important role memory can play in saving what most matters, cries out for such scenes to show that love, and even joy, senseless joy, are not antithetical to its rectitude. "It shuts out the world," as Trilling says, but there ought to be a fuller, more satisfied, and less barren sense of what is being shut in. Few hearts are going to leap up at the thought of Edmund and Fanny, and Kingsley Amis was not out of court when he asked if anyone would ever want to have dinner with them. But this is not the marriage of a prig to a mouse, and Austen could have tried to do better by them near the end. Mansfield is a place where speech, tone, action, and morality are to be present simultaneously in a single frame, all its considerations operating constantly; and when Austen is doing her slow unfolding, it is that. But when place is reduced to doctrine, it is only like most other doctrines.

Regardless of the ending, *Mansfield Park* could never escape seeming a willed idea. Northamptonshire was the right place to set it, but the setting was hard to sustain because it was too far away, too susceptible thereby to abstractness. No one had shown before how an excellent large book could be made out of the materials of a very small space, but it is a book that makes us want to desert our master and return to our friends. *Emma* is where Austen comes home, as it were, to her one book that really is about three or four families living in a village. Those who declare it Austen's masterpiece are, I think, responding to the ways it fulfills possibilities first glimpsed at Pemberley and sustained only with heroic tenacity at Mansfield.

Mary Mitford, as we have seen, blurs her memory of *Emma* into a generalization about all six novels. It is easy to do. Here is Raymond Williams describing Austen's communities:

Yet while it is a community wholly known within the essential terms of the novel, it is as an actual community very precisely selective. Neighbours in Jane Austen are not the people actually living nearby; they are the people living a little less nearby who, in social recognition, can be visited. What she sees across the land is a network of propertied houses and families, and through the holes of this tightly drawn mesh most actual people are simply not seen.

Of the six novels, *Emma* is the only one in which terms such as "a community well known" and "what she sees across the land" are at all useful, and Williams derives them from *Emma*. Yet in that novel we are most deeply absorbed in the question of neighbors—the Morlands, the Bennets, and the Elliots have no neighbors to speak of, the Dashwoods and the Bertrams each have one—many of whom are not part of "a network of propertied houses and families," and the whole matter of *Emma* is tied up with how we create the meshes through which we will see our neighbors.

To put the matter another way: One means something very different in saying of *Emma* that its world can be mapped than in proposing to do that in any of the other five novels. With the others no map of any small area is remotely possible, and one would be drawing lines on a map of the southern third of England to show the different places people live and visit. With *Emma* one wants a 1:25 Ordinance Survey Map to show the parishes of Highbury and Donwell, with an arrow at the edge pointing to Box Hill and another pointing to Richmond and London. With the exception of the excursion to Box Hill, the action of the novel is confined to a few square miles, and Emma herself, so far as we know, never has left and never will leave that area, not even for one night. Not surprisingly, then, in whatever way it is about "3 or 4 families," it has almost as many people in it as the other five novels combined. If actually making a map of *Emma*'s world seems a Janeite activity, the impulse to make one seems properly responsive to its central concerns. Rather than offer a map, I want to ask two questions, bearing in mind that this is the first time it is possible to ask such questions and expect reasonably accurate answers. Where do the Coles live? Where is the vicarage, the home of Mr. Elton?

In recent years the Coles have risen to be the second largest landowning family in Highbury parish. Since the Woodhouses at Hartfield are the largest, and Hartfield is only "a sort of notch in the Donwell Abbey estate," the Coles' holding need not be thought of as extensive, except it must be larger than Mr. Weston's at Randalls, and Mr. Weston has been doing well. When we finish sorting out places and approximate distances, it will be clear that the Coles probably have some land here and some there, scattered throughout the parish. Austen does not feel obliged to say where they live, not even when Emma goes there to dinner and there is dancing afterwards. We must therefore extrapolate.

Harriet Smith leaves Mrs. Goddard's one morning on a walk to Hartfield, and she stops to ask after a dress being made for her. It is raining when she comes out so she "ran on directly" to Ford's, "the first shop in size and fashion in the place," in Highbury high street. Harriet meets Robert Martin there, and after the shower is over he says she "had much better go round by Mr. Cole's stables, for I should find the near way floated by rain." The near way to Hartfield, presumably, is up the high street to the edge of the village, because at one point Mr. Weston stands at the gates of Hartfield and sees the rooms of Mrs. and Miss Bates, which are above a shop on the high street, near the Crown. If Hartfield is at the edge of the village, Mr. Cole's stables must be behind the village, and a track must run through the Coles' property for Harriet to walk on. We know from other evidence that Randalls is on the opposite side of the village from Donwell and the vicarage, and neither Harriet nor Mr. Martin mentions Vicarage-lane in giving and receiving directions; the Coles must therefore live on the same side of the village as Randalls and Hartfield, and Harriet would cross the road usually taken by the Westons and the Woodhouses when visiting each other.

That, admittedly, is a mouthful and tells us next to nothing about the novel. But it can be done. Austen liked to get her details right, and her details allow us to place the Coles, very minor characters in the novel, in a way we cannot begin to place the Harlowes, or Squire Allworthy and Squire Western. This exactness demonstrates what this novel does about its place that none other had done before. As for the vicarage, it is a quarter mile down Vicarage-lane from Highbury's high street. On the night Mr. Elton impetuously proposes to Emma, they are alone in a carriage leaving Randalls, and for no stated reason the carriage calls at the vicarage to drop Mr. Elton off before it goes on to Hartfield. Mr. Weston says he is afraid of a bad corner on the way, and, as we are told it is a half mile from Randalls to Hartfield and three quarters to the vicarage, the vicarage must be on the opposite side of the village from Randalls and Hartfield, and the bad corner is the junction of Vicarage-lane with the high street.

Something new has come into literature, and far from working with a tightly drawn mesh that screens out whomever one does not want to see, *Emma* may be the first book that seeks to saturate us in a place to such an extent that it can feel like the whole world. The people in this novel move within no more selective a mesh than most of us use all the time and, so far as we know, most people have always used. Of course Austen is no anatomist or sociologist of her created world, and, to be sure, she is not conversable with anyone whose rank is below that of the respectable tenant farmer. But in this world a single character, namely Emma herself, *might* confront anything at all within the confines of Highbury and Donwell, and we can say this because she does confront so much of it. "But where only one class is seen," Williams writes, "no classes are seen." What Emma faces is a world full of class consideration, some real and some imagined, and a world with lanes, weather, shops, and people one doesn't want to see that defies, or ignores, Emma's and Williams' obsessions about class. It says much when the best living Marxist literary critic can look at a novel that works to let in more than any book before had done only to start fussing about what it leaves out. We never do get the gypsies' names.

During the strawberry party at Donwell Abbey, Austen says the place yields "English verdure, English culture, English comfort," and some readers of *Emma* have been tempted to make this praise of Donwell emblematic of the book as a whole, thereby transforming village and manor into pastoral. But the example of Mrs. Elton is enough to put us on guard here; she does yield to that temptation, doting on this, being unable to get enough of that, trying to play a rural Marie Antoinette. Emma knows Highbury better than that, and we know that Emma is always in danger of being bored, which may count against her but speaks clearly about the smallness of her world. Princess of Highbury, there is nothing Emma cannot do, and she knows it, but we keep seeing there is little she *can* do, local meaning local, confined meaning confined.

Early in the novel, while Emma is consoling herself for the loss of Miss Taylor by planning a match between Harriet Smith and Mr. Elton, a sure sign of boredom, she and Harriet find the mid-December morning weather good enough to let them pay a visit to a poor sick family "a little way out of Highbury." Since Emma has shown no sign of being much interested in the poor, her reason for wanting to go does not become clear until we learn the route they must take:

> Their road to this detached cottage was down Vicarage-lane, a lane leading at right-angles from the broad, though irregular, main street of the place; and, as may be inferred, containing the blessed abode of Mr. Elton. A few inferior dwellings were first to be passed, and then, about a quarter of a mile down the lane rose the Vicarage; an old and not very good house, almost as close to the road as it could be. It had no advantage of situation; but had been very much smartened up by the present proprietor; and, such as it was, there could be no possibility of the two friends passing it without a slackened pace and observing eyes.—Emma's remark was—
>
> "There it is. There go you and your riddle-book one of these days." Harriet's was—
>
> "Oh! what a sweet house!—How very beautiful!—There are the yellow curtains that Miss Nash admires so much."

It is a painful moment. First Emma and then Austen must respond with a delicate touch, though with different aims in mind. Little in English literature before this novel could have instructed Austen how to create so much out of so little, and little could have instructed her readers in their best response.

An inferior lane with inferior houses that leads to an inferior vicarage, one Mr. Elton has helped little by smartening it up with, among other things, some dreadful yellow curtains. But of course Emma can say nothing of this since she has brought Harriet on this journey precisely so she will come to this spot and admire this prospect. Harriet, like the Mrs. Elton whose home it will be, loves it all, as Emma must both hope and fear. Emma herself is caught. She cannot in good conscience praise anything, but she brought Harriet here in order to feed her Emma-created fantasies:

> "I do not often walk this way *now*," said Emma, as they proceeded, "but *then* there will be an inducement, and I shall gradually get intimately acquainted with all the hedges, gates, pools, and pollards of this part of Highbury."

Emma cannot afford to be ironic, even if she knows that Harriet would fail to understand the irony, and what she says is at once precise, evasive, and monstrous. It is precise because it is true— if Harriet marries Mr. Elton then Emma will know much more than she now does about the hedges of Vicarage-lane. It is evasive because it conveys nothing of Emma's feelings about the vicarage and the vicar's taste. And it is monstrous because she can condescendingly believe she is being evasive for Harriet's sake.

Emma is trapped. Having chosen Harriet as her way to pass the time, she must accept what Harriet offers, and between Mr. Elton's yellow curtains and Harriet's exclamations over them, Emma is left no space. She can find nothing to admire in all this finagling of hers, and she is so isolated that only further stimulation from her imaginings can keep her in touch with society at all. Yet Highbury is not going to change and Emma is not going to leave, and if the village is not all tasteless vicars and wide-eyed girls, at this point it can be little else for Emma. If she jettisoned Harriet and Mr. Elton and all her fantasies about them, what would she have left? Austen is being very stern about place and what it grants to the village princess. Liking Emma is hardly the point; we need only see that she is more than a fantast with a need to impose her will on others. If we think for a moment about what Shakespeare does with Lady Macbeth, or what Fielding does with Lady Booby, then we see how original Austen is in making these "real" and distinctly unmetaphorical details work to achieve what earlier writers did by means of generalized or generalizing metaphor.

Seventeen chapters and some months later comes a moment of rare and precarious achievement, so little like anything else in Austen's fiction I feel inclined to think it strikes a personal note the way Peter Grimes's scene on the river seems to have done for Crabbe. Harriet Smith is in Ford's, and Emma, knowing how much Harriet dithers over every purchase, "went to the door for amusement":

> Much could not be hoped from the traffic of even the busiest part of Highbury;—Mr. Perry walking hastily by, Mr. William Cox letting himself in at the office door, Mr. Cole's carriage horses returning from exercise, or a stray letter-boy on an obstinate mule, were the liveliest objects she could presume to expect; and when her eyes fell only on the butcher with his tray, a tidy old woman travelling homewards from shop with her full basket, two curs quarrelling over a dirty bone, and a string of dawdling children round the baker's little bow-window eyeing the gingerbread, she knew she had no reason to complain, and was amused enough; quite enough still to stand at the door. A mind lively and at ease, can do with seeing nothing, and can see nothing that does not answer.

How is it that you live, and what is it that you do? So Wordsworth asks the leech-gatherer, seeking his own resolution and independence. The village dweller knows a similar problem, knows it not as a matter of "gladness" and "madness," but one of "nothing" and "enough," and Emma and Austen achieve, at the end of this passage, an equipoise that does not come with the territory.

The richness of Austen's description is offered within the frame of "Much could not be hoped" and "her eyes fell only," suggesting that there is a problem. The first phrase implies that Emma is being teased—*she* could not hope for much, spoiled princess that she is, yet the account of Highbury street life at its busiest shows that no one could hope for *much* here. Then, after "her eyes fell only" on Highbury not at its busiest, it turns out much *is* there: butcher, old woman, quarreling dogs, dawdling children. And this must therefore represent a challenge to Emma, a subtler one than that facing her with Harriet and the vicarage.

Emma, like everyone else, cannot be expected to find constant interest in things that must be at some distance, but if she can find no interest at all she is in trouble, because "most actual people," as Raymond Williams calls them, are there to be seen, must be seen, even by the princess of Highbury if she is ever to avoid the false stimulant of fantasy. Much earlier she has said Mr. Knightley is fond of "bending little minds," but we know by now that if Emma's mind is not bent it cannot save itself. So, seeing the butcher, the old woman, the dogs, and the children, "she knew she had no reason to complain," and, having no such reason and being reasonable, "was amused enough." Then comes a sentence of triumphant complexity: "A mind lively and at ease, can do with seeing nothing, and can see nothing that does not answer." There is "nothing" in this scene before Emma, and the richness of the detail does not deny the unremarkableness of each item taken by itself. Yet Emma's mind, lively and for once at ease, can move from the originally snobbish "Much could not be hoped," past "seeing nothing," and come to rest with seeing "nothing that does not answer." There is nothing too little for such a little creature as man, or woman; Emma has come a long way from the earlier scene in Vicarage-lane.

Austen keeps Emma's and our relation to these background matters active, forcing them to impinge on our consciousness not as clues to character understood as fixed quantity but as challenges and opportunities. As she deals with the smartened-up vicarage and Highbury high street, so she deals with Emma's relations with people close to her. Prone to boredom, Emma inflates Harriet, Mr. Elton, and Frank Churchill into objects of interest, and deceives herself about their faults and limitations. Fond of having her own way, she cuts herself off from Jane

Fairfax, a potential source of real interest, because Jane seems to threaten Emma's preeminent position. Undisciplined, she never does more than dabble at playing, drawing, or reading. If she is to avoid making a serious mistake, she must learn to live in her place. Shortly before the moment in the high street, Emma says, almost hysterically, to Mrs. Weston: "Mr. Knightley!—Mr. Knightley must not marry! I cannot at all consent to Mr. Knightley's marrying!" It takes many more chapters before "it darted through her, with the speed of an arrow, that Mr. Knightley must marry no one but herself!" That change is not the result of any change in Emma's relation to Mr. Knightley, but in her relation to her surroundings, which include the quarreling dogs, Miss Bates, Harriet, Jane, and much else that Emma does not want to see, but must learn to treat well, and does not know how to handle, but must learn to avoid weaving into a web of fantasy.

*Emma* is the Parthenon of fiction, writes Ronald Blythe, which seems quite right if by the term one means to imply a richness of detail, a clarity of design, and a tendency toward a limiting perfection in the final effect. The characters come and go in a neatly arranged fashion; the Emma-Harriet-Elton scene is fully enacted and just off the stage when Jane Fairfax and Frank Churchill arrive. When Frank leaves for the first time, Mrs. Elton conveniently appears, to strut, until he returns. It is the density and the dramatic relevance of its imagined place that sets this book apart, but it works against that density and that drama when the challenges to Emma turn out to be the challenges she needs, and in precisely the order in which she needs them, the simpler one first, the harder ones later. Most rigged in this regard is Austen's treatment of Mr. Knightley. Having decided that Mr. Knightley is no romantic hero but a wealthy improving farmer, Austen could place him in the landscape along with everyone else, and thereby make Highbury the seedbed of Emma's recognition that he must marry no one but herself. He gives the right answers all along, but she cannot see this until after she has blundered, been a false friend to Harriet, been rude to Miss Bates, snubbed Jane Fairfax, and learned she has done so. Because Mr. Knightley proposes precisely at the moment when Emma's education by mistakes can be called complete, he is put in the false position of announcing she has gotten full marks and he can therefore declare himself, a role more befitting a teacher than a lover. Austen had by this time mastered the art of plotting: there is here no awkward matching up of Marianne Dashwood to Colonel Brandon, no elopement of Lydia Bennet and Mr. Wickham to force Elizabeth and Darcy to settle their affairs, no hurrying of Henry Crawford into Maria Rushworth's arms. But Mr. Knightley is a rich creation, and he deserves more than being the one who asks "Is there a chance?" just when Emma has seen he must marry no one but herself. This is why saying that *Emma* is the Parthenon of fiction puts a limit on its achievement.

Yet *Emma* has a great claim on ordinary human affections, which are not entirely engaged in noting the carefully laid steps by which Emma grows up. Even in its most grimly ironic moments it is warm and loving in its way of saying that one has to live where one is. The butcher and the old woman outside Ford's can never come close to Emma, though her achieved equipoise in her moment with them should not be undervalued, but Miss Bates can, and learning how to deal with harmless bores is one of the great challenges of village life. Mr. Knightley's finest moment does not come when he lectures Emma at Box Hill, or when he proposes, but when he shows he knows how to live where he is:

"How is your niece, Miss Bates?—I want to inquire after you all, but particularly your niece. How is Miss Fairfax?—I hope she caught no cold last night. How is she to-day? Tell me how Miss Fairfax is."

And Miss Bates was obliged to give a direct answer before he would hear her in any thing else. The listeners were amused; and Mrs. Weston gave Emma a look of particular meaning. But Emma still shook her head in steady scepticism.

"So obliged to you!—so very much obliged to you for the carriage," resumed Miss Bates.

He cut her short with,

"I am going to Kingston. Can I do any thing for you?"

"Oh! dear, Kingston—are you?—Mrs. Cole was saying the other day she wanted something from Kingston."

"Mrs. Cole has servants to send. Can I do anything for *you*?"

Mr. Knightley has here the advantage of being a man, which means he can cut Miss Bates short as Emma and Mrs. Weston cannot, and which also means he is free to go to Kingston.

But no one of either sex in this novel can match the kindness of "Mrs. Cole has servants to send. Can I do any thing for *you*?" For as long as the moment lasts, it would be better to be Miss Bates than Mrs. Cole; it overturns rank and acknowledges it in the same gesture. Mr. Knightley knows who and where he is, his mind is lively and at ease, and his words here are a benchmark for himself and everyone else.

Highbury is a truly knowable community, a prison that yields a final sense that it can be made to seem world large enough. Austen's best work in this novel is in moments like those I've looked at here, whose little details uncover their relevance by showing the challenge of living in a small space, by hinting at the freedom that can come from truly accepting the challenge. *Emma* is a bold book because it tries to make much of what in another rendering would seem only trivial, but it is tactful in its boldness, needing to be precise in its locating of the spoiled princess inside the unimportant challenging surroundings. It is one of the most lived-in worlds in literature.

It won't do to call *Persuasion* autumnal, to compare it with Keats, to suggest it intimates Jane Austen's knowledge of her own imminent death. It was begun before *Emma* was ready for the press, it was finished in a year, long before there was any sign of the fatal illness, and far from being autumnal in tone, it is truly the happiest of her love stories. But it *is* quite different from the others and reveals a very different sense of life's possibilities. In *Persuasion* the stage is not bare, as it is in the early novels; place is subtly and carefully evoked to show that there is no place, no thing, no community, out there to take an interest in. This, coming after the richness of village life in *Emma*, may make it seem more discouraged and therefore more autumnal, when in fact Austen is assessing new ways to find one's way within the available space.

Kellynch is not a village but a hall with a small number of surrounding houses; it consists of five people—three Elliots, Lady Russell, and Mrs. Clay. Uppercross is a community of six people, all named Musgrove, and one satellite figure, Charles Hayter, a clergyman in a neighboring parish. The naval people, the Crofts, Captains Wentworth and Harville, Lieutenant Benwick, and Mrs. Harville, have no native habitat on land; they move about and some, we know, will settle somewhere, or anywhere. By the end of the novel only the Musgroves end up where they began. Everyone else is scattered about, and we never learn where Anne Elliot and Captain Wentworth go to live. At no point in the novel is there any feeling that people belong anywhere, are defined by where they are, or move comfortably in known domestic or domesticated space. The two places for which *Persuasion* is remembered are Lyme and Bath, resorts with rented dwellings and spas.

At the beginning of Chapter 6, after Kellynch has been let and Anne is getting ready to move:

> Anne had not wanted this visit to Uppercross, to learn that a removal from one set of people to another, though at a distance of only three miles, will often include a total change of conversation, opinion, and idea. She had never been staying there before, without being struck by it, or without wishing that other Elliots could have her advantage of seeing how unknown, or unconsidered there, were the affairs which at Kellynch-Hall were treated as of such general publicity and pervading interest; yet, with all this experience, she believed she must now submit to feel that another lesson, in the art of knowing our own nothingness beyond our own circle, was become necessary for her . . .

This is a new way to imagine space, as original in its way as what Austen created in *Mansfield Park* or *Emma*.

In *Pride and Prejudice* Netherfield is three miles from Longbourn, but Mrs. Bennet unquestioningly includes it in the magnetic field of her daughters. Sotherton is three times that far from Mansfield but stands in the role of neighboring estate, so that Sir Thomas can include the Rushworths among those he is willing to see as he otherwise closes his doors after the *Lovers' Vows* fiasco. Were Emma to go outside the parishes of Highbury and Donwell she might well have to learn a lesson in her nothingness beyond her own circle, but she is not going there, and inside her circle is a universe of people compared to Anne's Kellynch. To "become intimate with every spot and person" Kellynch contains would take half an hour.

Emma's task is to learn the way that the "nothing" surrounding her can and does answer; Anne's is to learn that it does not. When Captain Wentworth is absent from the novel, Anne's task is to endure lesser and greater evils. It is hard to say which of her sisters is worse, and most of the time she must live with one or the other. Lady Russell must be circumvented as much as respected. The Musgrove sisters ignore her, and her brother-in-law, Charles Musgrove, treats her as he would a governess. Bath is pretense and awkwardness. Space is mostly empty. No wonder the occasional moments of respite, like the autumnal walk, the arrival at Lyme, or the conversation with Lieutenant Benwick, stand out so strongly in the memory of the reader.

"She acknowledged it to be very fitting," the passage above goes on, "that every little social commonwealth should dictate its own matters of discourse." In the early novels it is presumed that people of a certain class can criss-cross the southern third of England without the slightest doubt that the conversation just ended at Norland, or Netherfield, can be picked up again easily at Barton, or Rosings, a hundred miles and more away. The presumption of Austen's letters is like this—conversable people can be found anywhere. This is not the case in the three Chawton novels. In *Mansfield Park* Edmund and Fanny must create a little social commonwealth in spite of his parents and everyone else, and the sense that there is something holy about this creation makes the process vital. In *Emma* smaller and larger commonwealths intersect and overlap, and the whole is defined, confined, known. In *Persuasion* the presumption of the early novels and the letters is the pretense of Sir Walter and Elizabeth Elliot, which is one reason Anne has for learning the art of her own nothingness. The landed class in this novel must turn to the navy for vitality, and even for decency, but none of the naval officers is interested in impeding the fragmenting process that dominates the book.

Of necessity in such a world, much depends on accident: the accident of the Crofts (Wentworth's sister and brother-in-law) renting Kellynch; the accident of Louisa Musgrove's fall from the Cobb, which replaces Wentworth with Benwick in her attention; the accident of Wentworth's overhearing Anne's conversation with Captain Harville, which prompts him to declare his love again. There is never any feeling that Anne, or even Wentworth, can do much to further their coming together, or that anyone else cares very much about what happens to either of them. The way place does not yield tone, meaning, or purpose is as carefully crafted here as the way it does produce these things at Mansfield and Highbury. Thus the patron saints of the novel are the Crofts, the couple that go anywhere, on sea or land, as long as they are together, the rest of the world not mattering. If we imagine them renting Netherfield, paying a visit to Mansfield, calling on relatives in Highbury—or becoming one of the summer residents, for that matter, at Sanditon in Austen's strange, uncompleted last novel—we realize how varied and different Austen's books are.

It is no coincidence that the first great woman writer in English appears at this time, this period of a new literature of place. Although Aphra Behn, Anne Finch, Fanny Burney, and Ann Radcliffe all led lives of at least somewhat wider scope than Austen's, they could do no more than offer versions of what men had done and done better. At the start of the nineteenth century, however, it became possible for a clergyman's daughter who spent her life in a few confined spaces to realize her immense talents by seeing that she had, within those spaces, materials rich enough to challenge her. Particular place was all, and Austen herself knew this, if only instinctively; and clearly she knew it most fully from 1810 on when she rewrote *Pride and Prejudice* and then wrote the three Chawton novels, each with its own place and sense of place, each with its own way of showing that the experience of limitation, particularity, and restriction is the experience of learning about freedom and intelligent moral choice. Women, presumably, had *known* that—had had to know that—for centuries, but it is only when someone knowing that is free to feel important that someone like Jane Austen can appear.

# IV

### ❧ WILLIAM COBBETT

COBBETT WROTE a shelf of books, including the *Political Register*, which once a week for many years offered itself as the political and economic conscience of England. He was born in 1763 and had a long career that to some looks like failure and to others like success. For instance, it is frequently said that Cobbett was the single person most responsible for the passage of the Reform Bill of 1832; he has admirers who feel he was wrong to settle for so little an achievement. Presumably because he is not "literary," he is missing from most anthologies of English literature, even one that devotes seventy-five pages to Carlyle. For students of literature he remains not someone to know so much as to know about.

Cobbett's most famous book is *Rural Rides* (1830), and we can restrict our attention to this volume because it represents his important contribution to the literature of place. But we will have to alter our bearings to show this. Cobbett had a home place that shaped him as much as any home place shaped anyone in this period, with the possible exception of Clare, and I will note more than once that Cobbett's outlook is nostalgic, his youth having given him all his essential standards of comparison. But he is a rural rider, a traveler whose places are ones he will be in today but not tonight or tomorrow, and this affects both the way he writes and the way we look at him. Though his sojourns are necessarily brief, Cobbett exudes confidence that from them he can learn the state and fate of England. He gives

65

us a chance to concern ourselves more with what was happening to the English countryside than we have thus far.

Cobbett's instinctive ambition was to speak for England, or at least for its conscience, its right knowledge. In the old culture the two voices that in theory could speak for England were those of the monarch and the church, but the basis of the claim was an understanding of symbolic, or magical, relations between monarch or clergy and the subjects, the sheep of the pasture. The execution of Charles I "ruined the great work of time," and after the Glorious Revolution a generation later the only ones who believed in magical relations between king and subjects were the loyal followers of the Stuart cause in the Highlands of Scotland. Elsewhere it was understood that the monarchy was an arrangement born of a series of accommodations among power groups; how else could it be understood if, at the time of the Hanoverian succession in 1714, there were fifty-seven people who had a better claim to the crown than did George I? What had been magic had become settlement, a matter of borrowing money and collecting taxes; the king not only could not speak for England but could not speak English. So too with the church and clergy. The great energies that built the cathedrals and the huge parish churches between 1100 and 1500 seemed able to unite and express a people, especially in comparison with events after the Reformation. After Henry VIII broke with Rome and the monasteries were closed, the crown gave their lands to its favored subjects, and gradually Anglicanism became a sect rather than a national church, and a persecuting sect at that; a great pastoral power was secularized into pious manners and a tithe-collecting arm of the propertied class. At the very least, then, if a voice *could* speak for England, it was not going to be one of the traditionally powerful voices, and, on the face of it, no unifying power larger than the human voice was there to serve as successor or replacement.

Traditionally, pastoral was the mode that expressed magical or symbolic relations, and by the eighteenth century it is not surprising to find an inability to understand how the hungry sheep could ever have looked up and *been* fed. Indeed, in his

66

denunciation of the church Milton still imagines that traditional language is viable, whereas a century later Johnson can imagine it is a relevant criticism of "Lycidas" that Milton and Edward King were never shepherds. Wordsworth calls "Michael" a pastoral poem because by the beginning of the nineteenth century "pastoral" had become a synonym for "rural"; the magical and symbolic relations are gone, and place has become particular and local.

If Cobbett had been told he sought to be a pastoral figure in the earlier sense of the term, he might well have concluded he was being addressed by "one of those frivolous idiots that was turned out from Westminster and Winchester School, or from any of those dens of dunces called Colleges and Universities," or perhaps someone from London, the GREAT WEN, "Jews, loan-jobbers, stock-jobbers, placemen, pensioners, sinecure people, and people of the *dead weight.*" The voice, clearly, is coarse, but in his time and place a certain coarseness may have been integral to his effort to harmonize the human and the natural and to denounce all that threatened that harmony.

*Rural Rides* is a journal of a number of journeys Cobbett took between 1822 and 1826 through the southern counties of England. He may have little bits of business to do here and there, but for the most part he rides because he wants to see and to report on what he sees, and he wants to take what he sees as evidence of what the state of England is, not just where he is but everywhere. He does not, of course, assume that the same thing is happening everywhere—no need to take journeys at all if that were so—but he always wants to interpret material facts as evidence and to read much into his interpretation. His crudeness is not the result of being afraid he will not be heard and has no hint of underlying defensiveness or uncertainty. It is part and parcel of his confidence. Thus it is unsurprising that he is given to superlatives; "Thus ended the most interesting day, as far as I know, I ever passed in all my life"; "Here I am, then, just going to bed after having spent as pleasant a day as I ever spent in my life"; "I never saw anything to please me like this valley of the Avon"; "It is impossible for the eyes of man to be fixed on a finer country than that between the village of Coxford and the town of Warminster"; in Warminster itself are "the finest veal and lamb that I had ever seen in my life," and a little farther on "there are the most beautiful trees that I ever saw in my life." As one might well imagine, when Cobbett turns that language on himself, he can be mightily pleased; "I got many blows in the sides, and if I had been either a short or a weak man, I would have been pressed underfoot and inevitably killed"; "During the whole of this ride I was very rarely abed after day-light; I drank neither wine nor spirits. I ate no vegetables, and only a very moderate quantity of meat." Though he never seems to see himself as a writer, he feeds on his own words.

In these excerpts Cobbett fills up too much of the space in his pictures, the natural surroundings and the human community serving as background for self-portraits in landscapes with low horizon lines, Cobbett and his horse dominating the scene. One might, seeing this, think how much more companionable is Defoe in his *Tour of England and Wales*, written about a century before *Rural Rides* and filled with much soberly presented lore and observation that seldom seeks to make more of what it offers than a local citizen would. But Defoe's modesty cannot guarantee that he can find enough for himself or for us to be truly interested in, because he is unable to connect, to point up relevance, to make his journey seem other than one place following another. There is, by comparison, hardly a page of *Rural Rides* that does not have its passionate outburst, its insistence that what happens to the land, and the people on the land, matters tremendously.

Many things feed this passion, one of which is Cobbett's skewed sense of history, without which he never could have proceeded so confidently or achieved so much. On their journeys, both Defoe and Cobbett come to Winchester, and both offer homage to William of Wickham, founder of Winchester Cathedral. I need not quote Defoe; his account characteristically is full of lore that Defoe need never have been in Winchester or seen its cathedral to report, place for him being a generator of lore. Here is Cobbett:

I took Richard to show him that ancient and most magnificent pile, and particularly to show him the tomb of that famous Bishop of Winchester, WILLIAM OF WYKHAM; who was Chancellor and the Minister of the great and glorious king, Edward III; who sprang from poor parents in the little village of WYKHAM, three miles from Botley; and who, amongst other great and munificent deeds, founded the famous College, or School, of Winchester, and also one of the Colleges at Oxford. I told Richard about this as we went from the inn down to the cathedral; and when I *showed him the tomb,* where the bishop lies on his back, in his Catholic robes, with his mitre on his head, his shepherd's crook by his side, with little children at his feet, the hands put together in a praying attitude, he looked with a degree of inquisitive earnestness that pleased me very much.

Cobbett is more personal than Defoe as he offers his recital of facts, but, more important, he senses a break with the past, believes in old magical relations that are gone now, and wants his son to understand history in terms of the contrast of past to present.

Up to this point in his story, Cobbett sees nothing to ignite him, but soon he gets what he needs:

The *"service"* was now begun. There is a *dean,* and God knows how many *prebends* belonging to this *immensely rich* bishopric and chapter: and there were, at this *"service," two or three men* and *five or six boys* in white surplices, with a congregation of *fifteen women* and *four men*! Gracious God! If WILLIAM of WYKHAM could, at that moment, have raised from his tomb!.... and had been told, that *that* was *now* what was carried on by men, who talked of the *"damnable* errors" of those who founded that very church!

So, when Richard says no one could make such a cathedral now, Cobbett replies: "That building was made when there were no poor wretches in England, called *paupers*; when there were no *poor-rates*; when every laboring man was clothed in good woollen cloth; and when all had plenty of meat and bread and beer."

69

Cobbett is right in saying that no one was called "pauper" and no one paid "poor-rates" in fourteenth-century England; no one did in the years of his youth either. But of course Winchester Cathedral was built at the time of the Black Plague, when good woolen cloth, meat, bread, and beer were neither in plentiful supply nor enough to prevent the deaths of a third of the population.

Decidedly Cobbett is a shortsighted historian; if he can remember (rightly or wrongly) something as having been true in his early years, he can insist it was always thus, and (always) when he sees a church that can seat a thousand people or a cathedral that can seat five thousand, he imagines that once these places were filled to capacity and infers that the total population of England has fallen since the Middle Ages. If this were all, his confidence would be only another name for pig-headed delusion, and Cobbett would only be offering ample evidence that in the early nineteenth century no voice could possibly claim, at least successfully, all that he claimed. But I think someone who had been more cautious about knowing the past would have been more cautious about knowing the present as well, and in Cobbett's case his active historical sense was food for his larger sense that the life of a society, of people, place, event, past and present, was intelligible, and this is what gave his rural rides, his descriptions of places where he would be today but not tonight or tomorrow, such impressive resonance. He looks at what Crabbe and Austen look at quite often, but where they claim that only small communities are knowable, he claims the ability to generalize from minutely observed evidence to the national scene.

Thus in the Isle of Thanet, in Kent, one of the richest wheat areas in England, Cobbett sees:

> The people dirty, poor-looking; ragged, but particularly *dirty*. The men and boys with dirty faces, and dirty-smock-frocks, and dirty shirts; and good God! what a difference between the wife of a labouring man here and the wife of a labouring man in the forests and woodlands of Hampshire and Sussex!

70

If this seems paradoxical, Cobbett can explain:

> Invariably I have observed that the richer the soil, the more destitute of woods; that is to say, the more purely a corn country, the more miserable the labourers.

That is acutely observed, and observation leads to generalization:

> The cause is this, the great big bull frog grasps all. In this beautiful island every inch of land is appropriated by the rich. No hedges, no ditches, no commons, no grassy lanes; a country divided into great farms; a few trees surround the great farmhouses. All the rest is bare of trees; and the wretched labourer has not a stick of wood, and has no place for a pig or a cow to graze, or even to lie down upon.

What his observation tells him is indeed the case, and the contrast between the rich corn country of Kent and the forests and woodlands of Hampshire and Sussex is enough to tell him why the laborers are dirtier and poorer in one area than the other.

Cobbett is right enough in one sense, but in fact there never had been hedges, ditches, common land, or grassy lanes in Kent, since the farms had been enclosed there when the land was first cleared, in the Middle Ages. He did not know this, and was inclined to think the great big bullfrog had been created in his lifetime. But this only means that here Cobbett had his history askew. The essential point about rich land yielding poor laborers remains intact, and, as a general rule, it can be said that when Cobbett is acute in his observations he will have at least something important to offer in his generalizations. He keeps his eyes on the object on this ride and therefore does not fall into two arguments he was fond of using, either of which would have betrayed his historical ignorance. He might have claimed that in olden times the laborers were more prosperous, and he might have claimed that it is London's rapacious demand for the countryside's produce that impoverishes these rural workers. Avoiding these, he rightly says that in areas farther west the land was poorer and therefore the cottagers lived better, because the landowners had not insisted upon a ruthless cultivation of the soil.

With Austen one is inclined to feel, for all her placing of some crucial scenes in Derbyshire and Northamptonshire where she had never been, that she seeks to write of what she knows on long acquaintance, and so too with Crabbe. Cobbett is in his rural rides a tourist—his book is travel literature, in effect—but, lacking Austen's or Crabbe's discretion, he draws more inferences from what he sees than they ever would. Thus, a few miles from the Isle of Thanet but still in Kent, he goes to Dover and scores wonderful direct hits:

> Here is a hill containing probably a couple of square miles or more, hollowed like a honeycomb. Here are line upon line, trench upon trench, cavern upon cavern, bomb-proof upon bomb-proof; in short the very sight of the thing convinces you that either madness the most humilating, or profligacy the most scandalous must have been at work here for years. The questions that every man of sense asks is: What reason had you to suppose that the *French would come to this hill*, to attack it, while the rest of the country was so much more easy to assail? . . . This is, perhaps, the only set of fortifications in the world ever framed for mere *hiding*.

The castle itself had been there since William I conquered the island by conquering its coastline, but in the two decades of the wars against France, 1793–1815, the land surrounding Dover Castle had indeed been fortified, as Cobbett says, "Just as if they would not go (if they came at all) and land in Romney Marsh, or on Pevensey Level, or anywhere else, rather than come to this hill."

The point of the observation is already clear, but we can note that in the observing Cobbett rises to a level of generalization that is not usual for Austen or Crabbe, and he follows it up by questioning Pitt and the others responsible for this folly: "The money must have been squandered purposely, and for the worst ends." He is one of the first to discover the secret of military expenditure in modern nations:

> What they wanted, was to prevent the landing, not of Frenchmen, but of French principles; that is to say, to prevent the

example of the French from being alluring to the people of England.

There, it seems to me, is the pastoral voice, the conscience, speaking. Cobbett assumes, rightly or wrongly, that the English had nothing to fear from French principles, but on seeing the fortifications at Dover he could insist that the country was thereby threatened with the loss of a harmony that existed before the money was "squandered purposely, and for the worst ends." Though I am unable to add to or subtract from this as an accurate historical account, I can say that the evidence offered by Wordsworth in *The Prelude,* by Coleridge in the *Biographia Literaria,* by Charlotte Brontë in *Shirley,* and by Elizabeth Gaskell in *Sylvia's Lovers* is ample and eloquent on the fierceness, the repressiveness, and the stupidity of the English in their fear of the French in the years during and after the French Revolution. It is out of the experience of these years, especially but far from exclusively as seen by Cobbett, that English radicalism was born. E. P. Thompson says: "It is as if the English nation entered a crucible in the 1790s and emerged after the wars in a different form."

Cobbett himself is not necessarily at his sharpest on the coast of Kent, where the fortification of Dover Castle practically hands him a vision of foreign policy seen from a single hill. He is not so much at home in Kent, whose countryside had been developed in its contemporary form many centuries earlier and did not show as many signs of the great growth of London as did Surrey and Hampshire. In his riding about these counties, Cobbett does not claim the special pride of knowledge he has of his home places, but his observation there is especially sharp and can show us most fully the possibilities and the limits of his ability to generalize from careful observation. Here he is at the sale of a farm in Surrey, only a few miles from where Emma Woodhouse faced the yellow curtains in Vicarage-lane in Highbury:

Oak clothes-chests, oak bedsteads, oak chests of drawers, and oak tables to eat on, long, strong, and well supplied with joint stools. Some of the things were many hundreds of years old. But all appeared to be in a state of decay and nearly of *disuse.*

There appeared to have been hardly any *family* in that house, where formerly there were, in all probability, from ten to fifteen men, boys, and maids: and, which was worst of all, there was a *parlour*! Aye, and a *carpet* and *bell-pull* too!

The crudeness here is muted, the nostalgia working to some point, so we know that Cobbett has found a true Cobbett place:

One end of the front of this once plain and substantial house had been moulded into a *parlour*; and there was the mahogany table, and the fine chairs, and the fine glass, and all as bare-faced upstart as any stock-jobber in the kingdom can boast of.

When one catches the scorn that lies behind that "mahogany table," in contrast with all the oak furniture being put up for sale, one sees also why SIR WALTER RALEIGH "was one of the greatest villains on earth," for introducing potatoes to England. England has no need of potatoes, or mahogany, and Lord knows how long the list might be extended; Cobbett could not distinguish Bishop Wilberforce from Dickens' do-gooding Mrs. Jellyby, because Wilberforce was raising a hue and cry about slaves when he should have been worrying about native English laborers.

But this *is* Cobbett at his best, and it is important not to become distracted:

And there were the decanters, the glasses, the "dinner-set" of crockery, and all just in true stock-jobber style. And I dare say it has been *Squire* Charington and the *Miss* Charingtons; and not plain Master Charington, and his son Hodge, and his daughter Betty Charington, all of whom this cursed system has, in all likelihood, transmuted into a species of mock gentlefolks, while it has ground the labourers down into real slaves. Why do not farmers now *feed* and *lodge* their work-people, as they did formerly? Because they cannot keep them *upon so little* as they give them in wages. This is the real cause of the change.

Think of Penshurst, and of Ben Jonson's celebration of magical relations between classes offered as a triumphant harmony, as if of people with nature—some of that lies behind Cobbett's scorn of what is for him a new establishment of class relations, snooty and aloof on the part of the owners. Once you create the parlor and the oak furniture goes into disuse, it follows that the laborers will no longer be fed and housed properly because the new class distinctions are based on cost effectiveness: "and yet so much does he gain by pinching them in wages that he lets all these things remain as of no use, rather than feed labourers in the house. Judge, then, of the *change* . . . and be astonished, if you can, at the *pauperism* and the *crimes* that now disgrace this once happy and moral England." He has probably gone too far, slid off into easier generalizing than in the previous passage, but remember, there are no longer agreed-upon ways and means of generalizing, and Cobbett has little to rely on to help him except instinct; so of course he can easily and frequently overstep himself, as when he is recalling, a latter-day John of Gaunt, "this once happy and moral England."

Cobbett excels at observation and at passionate bursts of generalization from observation, and that is why *Rural Rides* is better than most of the hundreds of issues of the *Political Register* and his various advice books. When he is out riding, there is always the possibility of a visual challenge that can turn the crude thinker into the pastoral knower. Faced with a book by Malthus or a speech by Canning, Cobbett knows so well what he thinks beforehand that he can never be more than momentarily impressive rhetorically; he just falls back on his preconceived opinion, facing no challenge. Even out in the countryside he had little of Defoe's ability to be simply interested in things. How did Dunwich fall, how was Lyme's harbor built, how far from London does London's marketing grasp extend—Defoe can ask these questions and be satisfied with the received answers. Faced with the same questions, Cobbett would tend to bluster, to make a point and not to worry if that point made little sense.

Thus when Cobbett sees churches too large for the existing population of a parish, he presumes that the population in these parishes was once large enough to fill the churches, a presumption so preposterous it makes one wonder what England would have been like had it been built from the beginning on Cobbett's principles. Cobbett then says England's population must therefore be declining—in fact, it doubled in Cobbett's lifetime—and that anyone who doubts this must be able to "literally believe, that *the moon is made of green cheese.*" There are other in-stances. Selborne Hanger, one of the highest hills Cobbett has seen, must consequently be "among the highest hills in En-gland," being in fact a quarter to a third the height of most of the bigger mountains in the Pennines and the Lake District. Or, if an area produces more food than it can eat, it is obvious that Quakers ("a sect of non-labourers") must be at work, since they are "as to the products of the earth, what the Jews are to gold and silver."

These are the consequences of Cobbett's pulling the trigger too quickly, as he also was wont to do even when his clearest observation led to some of his richest generalizing. We have looked at his insights about rich land and poor workers, about the fortifications against French ideas, about the Charington parlor and mahogany table. He might have asked himself how all these were related, but to do that would have required a sense of history that Cobbett did not have; for him it was enough to treat landscape as text and to follow with sermon. In fact, and these were not facts totally unavailable to Cobbett, London had been a Great Wen well before he was born; the capitalist system he saw invading the countryside had been expanding, and cre-ating and defining the landed gentry, for two centuries and more, so that what Cobbett saw was neither new nor so impressively expanding as to be news just then.

There had been a huge inflation in farm prices and a corre-sponding rise in farm rents during the years of the Napoleonic wars. After Waterloo prices fell but rents did not; many land-owners were therefore squeezed and became inclined to squeeze their workers, especially if they had undertaken the considerable expense of enclosing their land in false expectation of prices' remaining high. As a result the 1820s, the decade of *Rural Rides*, was one of the worst ever for rural workers, and the situation was not helped by the great shifting in land ownership through-out the period, which meant that many new owners like Henry Crawford had never known a relation between land, owner, and worker that was not capitalist.

Cobbett could see some of this at least, but he saw it either as a single great blob called London, or as little bits that could not be synthesized into a single view no matter how hard he tried, or as a matter of England's needing nothing so much as a return to the time of Cobbett's youth. The blob was the WEN, London, run by the THING, and the THING controlled England by means of rotten boroughs, paper money, taxes, poor laws, national debt, standing armies, and the granting of power to the likes of Dissenters and Jews. In the place of analysis Cobbett made lists, especially of villains, but the flaw of drawing up lists and of hurling words into block capitals was that they suited Cobbett's temperament all too well and thereby rendered his shrewd perceptiveness quiescent.

"Here I am, in Kent and Christendom," wrote Thomas Wyatt to his own John Poins three centuries earlier. It is a way of speaking Cobbett loved, for it places the voice at the center of the universe. But much had changed in three centuries. Wyatt speaks from a generalized place and feels no need to comment on the particular place; "Kent" is a part of Christendom as good as any other, and as long as it stands apart from the court it is an address from which letters are written. Knowing a place, in our sense of the term, was seldom relevant. A familiar place provided material, lore, and suggested the best available metaphor, but places never demanded perceptive scrutiny of particulars. "Kent" for Cobbett, though, *is* its own place, not a generalized one, and to the extent that he wanted or needed to separate Kent from the rest of Christendom, to say how its farms and people were different from those in Sussex and Hampshire, to that extent the generalizations he could make about one place were restricted to that place, as surely as Gilbert White's observations and generalizations about the behavior of sand martins and swallows applied only to them and not to nightingales, to say nothing of squirrels. To that extent Cobbett was always on dangerous ground when he tried to look at a place and intone about the fate of England. In its early stages, his generalizing is often wonderfully good. It is in moving from the particulars and his early generalizations to his attempts to state larger conclusions that he most often gets into trouble, falling back on his prejudice or his shortsighted sense of history.

The task he had given himself, however, was difficult, more

difficult than he knew, certainly. What helps Cobbett is his love of details, and this keeps him from trying to generalize without regard to anything local or particular. As for what might happen when such a thing was attempted, take these lines of Wordsworth's:

> Milton! thou shouldst be living at this hour:
> England hath need of thee; she is a fen
> Of stagnant waters: altar, sword, and pen,
> Fireside, the heroic wealth of hall and bower,
> Have forfeited their ancient English dower
> Of inward happiness.

It would be interesting to juxtapose "On the late massacre at Piedmont" to see Milton mixing the general with the particular. But here it is enough to say that it does not help us, or Wordsworth, to call this poem "London, 1802" because it remains all stance, attitude, vague gesture. By some unknown process halls, bowers, and firesides lose "inward happiness" and thereby become fens, and Milton, of all people, is called upon to observe or reverse this miracle of catastrophe. It is a poem that needs space and time coordinates, and something like Cobbett's shrewd eyes, to keep it from being mumbo-jumbo, feeling and bluster. We will have ample occasion later to see what wonderful generalizing Wordsworth could do when starting from haunting particulars, but even great writers are at risk when they fail to see how things change, history happens, and the possibilities for successful utterance thereby are altered.

Jane Austen offers splendid confirmation. Because we often understand her as the heir of Dr. Johnson, our instinct may tell us to think of her as a novelist given to more generalizing than later writers. But her most famous generalization belongs to the feeble understanding of Mrs. Bennet, and ironically, despite her husband's ridicule, Mrs. Bennet's statement about single men in possession of a good fortune is perhaps the only generalization that all six novels uphold. Except for that one, if we think of the subjects in which Austen shares an interest with Cobbett, such as money, class, property, or London, it is surprising to note that she, like him, is always confident but, unlike him, avoids generalizations and makes it difficult for others to generalize about her. She shares Cobbett's feelings about London, presumably, but her only characters who actually live there, the Gardiners and John and Isabella Knightley, are just about everyone's, including Austen's, favorite minor characters in her fiction. Her clergymen are a mixed lot: Henry Tilney, Edward Ferrars, William Collins, Edmund Bertram, Philip Elton, and Charles Hayter. Her improving landowners are Mr. Rushworth, Henry Crawford—and George Knightley. Her titled aristocrats are dreadful—Lady Catherine de Bourgh, Sir Thomas Bertram, Sir Walter Elliot—but her greatest hero is aristocrat in all but title. Her new-rich are Augusta Hawkins—and Frederick Wentworth. In the four major novels the social range from top to bottom is large, but no class or profession, and no attitude about money, learning, travel, or society outside the family is built up as a structure of emphasis or preference we can call Austen's own. Of course there are generalizations in her fiction, but I think scrutiny would show that they are mostly dramatic, offered as hypotheses rather than received truths. It may well be that those who have found her narrow because she ignores the rural poor or the Napoleonic wars are in fact responding to her variousness, which demands from her readers an absorption in this time and that place that makes generalization difficult.

The shift we have been following, from the generalized to the particular place, turns out to have little-seen consequences, one of the most important being the shift in the nature of generalizing, in the structure of successful generalization. To look at almost any twenty or thirty lines of a Shakespeare play is to see speeches that move back and forth from the detailed to the generalized as if the act were as simple as breathing:

Give me a cup of sack, rogue—Is there no virtue extant?

My lord, here are letters for you—
O gentlemen, the time of life is short . . .

The queen, my lord, is dead.
—Tomorrow, and tomorrow, and tomorrow . . .

79

The movement from detail to generalization is easy enough, but the presence or absence of sack does not mean there is, or is not, any virtue extant. We cannot say of these generalizations that they succeed or fail. Nor is the situation much different if we start with the generalizations, as with "The quality of mercy is not strained" or "To be or not to be." Modern readers have learned to distinguish detail, or particular, from generalization, and we have to work to learn that in earlier centuries that distinction was much less clearly defined or felt. In our period, the transition between then and now, it may be said that for the first time it became possible for a generalization to fail.

"A mind lively and at ease," Austen writes, "can do with seeing nothing, and can see nothing that will not answer." Cobbett, hearing this, would have ground his teeth. *His* mind could never do with seeing nothing and could never imagine it was nothing that he was seeing, because his perception must answer to his mind's need to be lively and to know the meaning of what he is seeing. In these circumstances he must generalize, and it is possible for the generalizations to fail.

Cobbett is in Whiteflood, on the Hampshire downs—"These hills are amongst the most barren of the Downs of England; yet a part of these was broken up during the rage for improvements." The result was a disaster—"A man must be mad, or nearly mad, to sow wheat on such a spot." If not strictly true, it is fair enough, and Cobbett, had he been asked, could have given the farmer warning. But here is Cobbett's conclusion:

> And this was *augmenting the capital of the nation.* These new enclosure-bills were boasted of by George Rose and by Pitt as proofs of national prosperity! When men in power are ignorant to this extent, who is to expect anything but consequences such as now we behold.

From a madman to a mad nation. It does not work, but it is important to ask why.

"Improvements, Ma'am!" is Cobbett's shorthand term of contempt for enclosures, and it is hardly surprising that agriculturalists, enclosure commissioners, and surveyors all had a bad smell for him, since they were a new sort of person and were

80

not satisfied with the England of his youth. The very idea that the capital of the nation could be increased sounded fishy to him, like paper money. In an 1813 *Political Register* he objected to a general enclosure law because he was sure it was not possible to increase the food supply without increasing the population. So he is pleased to note the failure of the mad Hampshire farmer's ploughed downland because it "proved" that enclosure, which in this case would have allowed sheep or cattle to be removed from the land, could not augment the capital of the nation. It can be presumed that in the particular case Cobbett could have been right, but in the general case he was quite wrong. The wealth of the nation increased greatly during the period of the greatest enclosures, and because of them in part: not so much in Hampshire as elsewhere, not so much or so quickly as many enclosers hoped, and not so much by the single act of enclosing as by the accompanying changes in husbandry, crop rotation, ditching, and drainage. Cobbett is a farmer, he sees the broken-out land and the poor yield, and, not content to say the farmer is a fool, he generalizes, and suddenly enclosures in Norfolk, Leicestershire, and Yorkshire, all successful and all unknown to Cobbett, are the work of fools. Surely they must be—since here is Cobbett, in Hampshire and Christendom, is he not?

I do not intend to scorn so much as to indicate the precariousness of the enterprise, and I need to end with what I take to be a brilliant sequence showing how, in the period when generalizing itself was becoming more perilous, Cobbett could relate observation to generalization splendidly. Cobbett's ride down the valley of the Avon to Salisbury, on August 30, 1826, in which he is retracing a route he had taken almost twenty years earlier, yielded one of his finest sustained pieces of writing. The following may need a larger context to show all its strengths, but it clearly shows the shrewd eye of the superb early classifier and generalizer:

I found the place *altered* a good deal; out of repair: the gates rather rotten; and (a very bad sign!) the roof of the dog-kennel falling in! There is a church, at this village of Netheravon, large

81

enough to hold *a thousand or two* of people, and the whole parish contains only 350 men, women, and children. This Netheravon was formerly a great lordship, and in the parish there were three considerable mansion-houses, besides the one near the church. These mansions are all down now; and it is curious enough to see the former *walled gardens* become orchards, together with other changes, all tending to prove the gradual decay in all except what apertains merely to *the land* as a thing of production for the distant market.

Until this last phrase, it is unclear what direction Cobbett intends to take, but the observation is clear and shrewd, so the yield should be rich; Cobbett can "see" decay in the fallen-in roof of the kennel and paradoxically also in the productiveness of the orchards.

"But indeed, the people and the means of enjoyment *must go away.*" Most writers, including Cobbett himself when less alert, would have written "employment" rather than "enjoyment," and thereby lose the sense that what the walled gardens as well as the kennel are concerned with is not productivity but quality of life:

> They are drawn away by the taxes and the paper-money. How are *twenty thousand new houses* to be, all at once, building in the WEN, without people and food and raiment going from this valley towards the WEN? It must be so; and this unnatural, this dilapidating, this ruining and debasing work must go on, until that which produces it be destroyed.

This may not be entirely clear. Earlier in his account of this day, Cobbett insists that "though paper-money could CREATE nothing of value, it was able to TRANSFER everything of value." Further, he had noted that the women of this valley once had full employment carding and spinning wool, and their work had ceased with the widespread use of the spinning jenny and the factories to house it.

Here Cobbett sees what he often is blind to elsewhere, that a decline in rural population did not mean a decline in national population but a transfer of people; and the kennel, the disappearance of the three mansion houses, and the appearance of orchards where walled gardens had been are all observations leading to the generalization about rural neglect, loss of enjoyment, and transfer of wealth and people to the WEN, where twenty thousand new houses were being built. About London itself Cobbett may have been shortsighted, because his WEN was the city being built by John Soane and John Nash, but he is dead right about the relation of Netheravon to London. If, as Cobbett suspects, the disappearance of the mansion houses and walled gardens was the result of enclosures, then his point about the effects of a new kind of people coming to the countryside is secure. Crabbe speaks often about the difference between the sloppy old farmer who had a good relation with the people on his land and the classy efficient new farmer who is all capitalism and productivity. And what Crabbe notes in his fine wry way, indicating a value but not raising his voice, is food and drink to Cobbett. Even Crabbe would not have seen the dog kennel as revealingly as Cobbett does.

All this is to say that Cobbett at his best can sound a note that Jane Austen cannot. She is seldom foolish, especially in the folly of generalizing, because she is so carefully absorbed in her people of this time and that place. But such absorption did not affect her assumption that money and land were simply different forms of wealth; and if there ever was a relation of land, landowner, and worker that was not capitalist, she neither knew nor cared. It can be said for Cobbett that he has just enough history, along with a different and richer sense of the countryside than Austen's, to yield him a much more resonant sense of the value of land, and of people working with it and on it, than she could possibly have. Her confidence lies in her absorption, in the sense of intimacy of places; Cobbett's lies in his wonderfully interpreting observations, and what they lead him to, wrong and wrong-headed though his points of rest often are. Thus her fiction had no successors, in part because her generalizations broke down as they were supposed to do and yielded only the local truths they could. Raymond Williams is right to suggest that Cobbett's attempts to generalize about land, class, and money are precursors of the fiction of George Eliot and Hardy; what Cobbett reached to conclude about the new and the old relations to land, and the classes of people engendered by the new relations, is appropriated by the novelists as rich material for their fictions.

Cobbett is crude, Cobbett is a little-Britain bigot, Cobbett is a biased historian and, quite often, a desperate generalizer. Yet Cobbett is the first major voice of modern English radicalism, and radicalism has played an important and distinguished role in English thought and letters. The problem is not so much that of deciding which aspect is the most in need of being stressed as that of trying to write about him from a point of view different from that of most of the people who have so carefully preserved his memory. It is a great shame that he is so little known except as part of that radical tradition. An admiring but unradical American would like to make Cobbett's writing known and his presence felt among many to whom he is merely a name that begins with C and isn't Cowper, Clare, or Crabbe, and to admit to feeling ambivalent about him in ways his radical heirs need not feel.

"I have never gone out to 'take a walk' in the whole course of my life," Cobbett writes, striking a characteristic pose, "nor to take a ride; there had to be something to make me take one or the other." I tend to feel combative about such swaggering, knowing that he is one person and I another. I could, I answer, simultaneously take a walk and have something to make me take one: something, indeed, like *Rural Rides.* I could walk a rural ride, avoid Hindhead, stop at the Holly Bush in Headley, note the scrabbly common land nearby that both Cobbett and Defoe found shocking.

The two signs I love most in England and miss in America are those that announce a pub and those that proclaim a Public Footpath. In accepting their announcements and proclamations, especially in places in the southern counties well known to Cobbett, I have come to hear a voice, blustery and outraged:

Public footpath! Gracious God, could there be a clearer sign that the WEN keeps moving, out from its center, by *taking a walk,* no less. And why? Because some nabob, or stock-jobber, some pensioner or admiral, has taken over a perfectly good farm. In the wake of all his Improvements, Ma'am, he has the gall to announce just where our feet and the hooves of our horses can be put, and if any decent traveler might want to trample his corn. The tide moving out from the WEN may think it is being "nicely treated," thank you, by this sign of PUBLIC FOOTPATH, but when the nabob restricts the common right to one puling track, the beast will soon want to remove the track as well.

And then:

In any decently regulated country, one finds public houses, and travelers know their gratitude for them. But here is THE WHITE HORSE, a sign painted by a man showing in every stroke of the brush that he had never seen the same, at least could not tell it from THE WHITE HART! Pretty signs indeed! To delight the Tourists that now crowd into the turnpikes. So people are *hired* to entice those who lately left a decent countryside and who now desire to visit it *on holiday*, to leave the WEN and to mar the land with these "signs" of public accommodation and national ignorance. And who, visiting these coaching inns, knows that wherever the cottager has ceased to make his own beer, in that place "Improvements, Ma'am!" have invaded. So we have ever-so-pretty signs saying THE GREEN MAN by those who do not know the man, and others nearby announce the ruin of the country with their sign of PUBLIC FOOTPATH.

Walking from Selborne to Thursley, along the route of a Rural Ride, I cleverly give Hindhead a miss, as Cobbett has instructed. But I love the Holly Bush in Headley, which he hated, and what, I wonder, would be his response to my spending the night at the Pride of the Valley, a Best Western Hotel, right outside the Thursley that Cobbett always liked? How to placate his ghost, since the Pride of the Valley caters to outgrowths from the WEN and I pay for my lodging with a credit card? Gracious God!

The walk ends in Farnham, at what was the Jolly Farmer, on Bridge Street, where the man himself was born. It is now called

The William Cobbett, and is filled with small rooms housing video games, and television sets which blink the Pages from Seefax. During a Happy Hour I was served a hamburger covered with an excellent Stilton sauce. Except for the portrait of Cobbett on the sign, one finds little trace of the master, and, given the noise, it is hard to hear, though easy to listen for, the sound of Cobbett rolling over in his grave.

# V

## ❧ JOHN CLARE

THE BICENTENNIAL of John Clare's birth approaches, and it is still difficult to see him steadily or whole. His first publisher, John Taylor, printed his poems with punctuation and language not Clare's own, and this practice did not begin to cease until a generation ago. Anthologies frequently distort him this way, and also by concentrating on the later "madhouse" poems. Some of his poems have never been published in any form, and the long-promised Oxford edition by Robinson and Powell has yet to appear. One of the major poetry events of the last twenty years, the publication of the huge *Midsummer Cushion* in 1978, took place but few noticed, and the book is going out of print in Britain without ever having been published in America. As a result, Clare's strong admirers have often seemed to be making an ado about something, but what is not clear. "A third-generation Romantic," a friend of mine tagged Clare. Clare was born in 1793, a year after Shelley and two before Keats, and all attempts to squeeze him into some category of Romantic have failed, often with the trailing implication that that means he is lesser for not being Romantic. It is all a shame.

Clare is one of the most distinctive writers about a place who ever lived. A combination of circumstances helped make him so. One of these was the enclosure of his native parish of Helpston in Northamptonshire (now in Cambridgeshire), which radically altered the landscape he knew as a child. Another was the entirely well-meant, interfering advice and editorial alterations of his London publisher, John Taylor. Each of these was a blow, and they might well have diminished or defeated a different or a lesser person. They were refiner's fire for Clare's poetry.

In 1832, when Clare was thirty-nine, he and his family moved from the cottage in Helpston that had always been his home to one in Northborough, only three miles away. He then wrote two of his most composed and polished poems, "Decay" and "The Flitting," about the strong sense of displacement he felt after moving—"The summer like a stranger come / I pause and hardly know her face"—and it has sometimes been suggested that Clare was so tied to Helpston that he could not go even three miles away without feeling like Mowbray in *Richard II*, banished to the frozen Caucasus. The actual situation was different. In his teens and twenties Clare moved freely within the land between the rivers Welland and Nene, which divided his part of Northamptonshire from Lincolnshire on the north and Rutland and Huntingdon on the south. He was not always strong enough to hire himself out as a field laborer, and so he moved about, picking up other jobs. When working for the Blue Boar in Helpston he made weekly visits for flour to Maxey, two miles to the north; he worked for a year as a gardener on the huge Burghley estate five miles to the west, and when he left that job he wandered as far north as Grantham and Newark; he worked at a lime kiln in Pickworth, south of Helpston, and courted Martha Turner in Bridge Casterton. He frequently went to Stamford to buy books and first arranged for publication of his poems with a bookseller in Market Deeping. When he then made his first visits to London, and was in the company of Taylor, Hazlitt, Lamb, and others associated with the *London Magazine*, he was not seen as some country clown crippled by birth, birthplace, or current station. No one ever took Clare for a citizen of the world, but he was not on the edge of collapse whenever he left his native parish, and we must account for "The Flitting" and "Decay" in other ways.

When he was "very young," Clare writes in his *Autobiography*, he was often alone and "felt a curiosity to wander about spots where I had never been";

So I eagerly wanderd on & rambled among the furze the whole
day till I got out of my knowledge when the very wild flowers
and birds seemd to forget me & I imagind they were the inhabitants of new countrys the very sun seemd to be a new one &
shining in a different quarter of the sky still I felt no fear my
wonder seeking happiness had no room for it.

That is a marvelous description, but the event it describes is so
much like any child's first straying as not to seem remarkable.
To be out of his knowledge was a wonder, not a fear. He saw the
sun go down and returned home, where everyone was worried
about him.

Compare this with a stanza from "The Flitting," about the
move to Northborough, made more than thirty years after the
childhood jaunt and a decade after the *Autobiography*:

Alone & in a stranger scene
Far from spots my heart esteems
The closen with their ancient green
Heaths woods & pastures sunny streams
The awthorns here were hung with may
But still they seem in deader green
The sun een seems to loose its way
Nor knows the quarter it is in

"I dwell on trifles like a child," he begins the next stanza, but
these are hardly trifles. In both passages, in a strange place the
sun shines in a different quarter of the sky, and the similarity of
wording underscores the contrast between a thrilling childhood
exploration and a deeply felt displacement at forty. That he
should use the same expression about the sun, though, shows
only that it was an image for him, a way of stating differences
more than a way of looking at the sky. What is hard to account
for is the deep melancholy the phrase conveys in "The Flitting,"
as if Helpston and Northborough were entirely different landscapes. In fact Northborough, closer to the fenland of the Wash,
has fewer trees and no equivalent of Emmonsailes Heath, where
the land rises southwest of Helpston and goes "out of knowledge." And Clare seems seldom to have gone in the direction of

Northborough before he moved there. But none of this comes close to explaining such a strong feeling of dislocation, "Alone & in a stranger scene."

My sense is that the move really only brought to new and full articulation feelings Clare had known for years. Northborough was "far from spots my heart esteems" because, in 1832, Helpston itself was not the village of his early years, so he was, on leaving it, only continuing a journey he had begun years earlier. In another poem written in or near 1832, "Remembrances," Clare writes of two other losses sustained besides the loss of his native home. First, the loss of innocence and youth, expressed in a familiar nostalgia:

When I used to lie & sing by old eastwells boiling spring
When I used to tie the willow boughs together for a "swing"
& fish with crooked pins & thread & never catch a thing
With heart just like a feather—now as heavy as a stone
When beneath old lea close oak I the bottom branches broke
To make our harvest cart like so many working folk
& then to cut a straw at the brook to have a soak
O I never dreamed of parting or that trouble had a sting
Or that pleasures like a flock of birds would ever take to
        wing
Leaving nothing but a little naked spring

Though two places, "eastwells boiling spring" and "old lea close oak," are mentioned here, this is mostly generalized experience in generalized place, like Clare's straying from home as a child; that does not keep it from being a poignant moment for Clare, his heart "as heavy as a stone," but it has no stamp of a particular place.

The second loss, though, has its time and space coordinates fully expressed:

By Langley bush I roam but the bush hath left its hill
On cowper green I stray tis a desert strange & chill
& spreading lea close oak ere decay had penned its will
To the axe of the spoiler & self interest fell a prey
& crossberry way & old round oaks narrow lane

With its hollow trees like pulpits I shall never see again
Inclosure like a buonoparte let not a thing remain
It levelled every bush & tree & levelled every hill
& hung the moles for traitors—though the brook is
   running still
It runs a naked brook cold and chill

This was written a dozen years after the enclosures in Helpston had changed its landscape, but clearly Clare was still riveted, still looking and seeing what was and what is. No hill larger than a molehill had in fact been leveled, but Clare knew that if the moles were trifles, so was he, his characteristic line of sight being close to the ground. The Napoleons who had cleared land and removed trees could treat both Clare and the moles as vermin. The landscape is so particularized that without knowing it from other writings of his one might not guess that "spreading lea close" and "round oaks" are names of places.

These two laments, for a lost youth and for a pre-enclosed world, had persisted as active cries years after Clare first felt and expressed them, and it seems important to bear them in mind as losses or displacements from which he did not recover; he had, in that sense, been on his way to Northborough for twenty years or more. The last passage here ("Inclosure like a buono-parte") is often cited as part of Clare's attack against enclosures, but the attack is really a lament, more personal than political or satiric, and so it usually is in Clare's writing. (Just to keep some background comparisons clear: Cobbett of course was often political and satiric, but, concerning enclosures, his was a different world. In southeastern England almost all enclosing had been completed much earlier, and it was only a mad farmer's ruined downland or scrabbly common that Cobbett saw. In much of the midlands large-scale enclosing took place primarily within the years of Cobbett's and Clare's lifetimes.)

Many of us have had similar experiences of seeing childhood scenes disappear—trees, fields, paths, older building replaced by new houses, highways, shopping centers. Each generation, furthermore, seems to train its eyes to be offended by changes particular to that generation. Thus when I went to Helpston, I was immediately bothered by the long row of houses that stretches aimlessly between Helpston and Glinton and damages the compactness of the village, even the identity of the parish. Clare's cottage, by the very fact that it has a plaque and is being handsomely kept up, seems more like Ye Olde John Clare House than the home he lived in. Council houses have replaced fields to the southwest of the village within living memory. For real awfulness, one need go no farther than Pickworth and Castor, a few miles to the south, where Clare worked at the lime kiln and courted Martha Turner. The bulldozers are hard at work extending the hideous development of Bretton (itself immortalized in the Janet Bird sections of Margaret Drabble's *The Realms of Gold*), north from Peterborough. Sensitive to such current dangers and disasters, we can look at the prosperous fields around Helpston and find it hard to believe it was *that* which cut Clare off from his childhood and felt to him like the loss of innocence. In trying to reconstruct Clare's experience, we need to learn to be offended by square fields, hedgerows, drainage ditches, and carefully grown plantations of deciduous trees.

That Clare was short, slender, and physically never cut out for a life of constant heavy labor may have contributed to his setting himself, even as a boy, somewhat apart. He describes games he played with others, but then adds "I never had much relish for the pastimes of youth." Rather than play football on a winter Sunday, he read, and in the warmer months he seems mostly to have been by himself, working by shepherding or scaring birds, developing his wonderful powers of observation, getting himself down to the level of the molehill, the nightingale's nest, the snipe in the marsh, the beetle, the mouse. Beatrix Potter was also uncommonly observant of the life of small things, and she too spent most of her early years alone; her creatures, though, inhabit enclosed spaces, because she did, and Clare's are free and open, because his life was. Here is his sand martin:

> Thou hermit haunter of the lonely glen
> & common wild & heath—the desolate face
> Of rude waste landscapes far away from men
> Where frequent quarrys give the dwelling place
> With strangest taste & labour undeterred
> Drilling small holes along the quarrys side

More like the haunts of vermin than a bird
& seldom by the nesting boy descried
Ive seen thee far away from all thy tribe
Flirting about the unfrequented sky
& felt a feeling that I cant describe
Of lone seclusion & a hermit joy
To see thee circle round nor go beyond
The lonely heath & its melancholly pond

As so often in Clare, the human is at a distance in this poem, not something he feels cut off from but not something he is part of either. The only person not far away is the "nesting boy," a lad good at finding nests, perhaps, but he may not know, as Gilbert White noted and Clare knows, that the sand martin is "very defective in architecture." Yet both Clare and the bird, for all they are out in the glen or on the heathland common, are in a circumscribed space. The "hermit joy" is a feeling one gets when one does not go beyond "the lonely heath and its melancholly pond." Clare seldom goes out of his knowledge, and he is usually a solitary, looking at other solitary things.

He began writing poems very young, and for a long time that too was a fugitive activity. He imitated his father's ballads, and at one stage would read his poems aloud to his parents while holding a book open so they would not know he was reciting his own work. He loved reading—Thomson, Gray, Goldsmith, Chatterton. The earliest surviving poems, unsurprisingly, and indeed many of those in his first volume, which made him famous, show the avid reader more than the haunted lover of the heath:

Winter's gone, the summer breezes
  Breathe the shepherd's joys again,
Village scene no longer pleases,
  Pleasures meet upon the plain.

Or this:

Sweet tiny flower of darkly hue,
  Lone dweller in the pathless shade;

93

> How much I love thy pensive blue
>   Of innocence so well displayed.

It is poetry that could as easily have been written in London as Helpston.

This is true of "Helpstone," where we first hear about the ravages of enclosures, because the poem is so completely imitative of Goldsmith's "Deserted Village" that Clare incorporates Goldsmith's confusion into his own poem. Clare here has Goldsmith's difficulty distinguishing among losses, among things to be lamented, and among responses to loss. He begins by saying that the point about Helpston is that it is obscure, unknown to grandeur or to fame, and that he himself is poor. This leads to lamenting his lost boyhood, and that, in turn, leads to a lament for trees that have been beheaded and bushes that have been uprooted by improving enclosers. There follow ten lines that denounce "accursed Wealth"; two victims of wealth are "our loss of labour and of bread" and "my dear green willows," but it is unclear how the losses are related or whether he thinks they are. So, when he ends the poem saying he wants to die in Helpston, the place he seems to have in mind is the one he insists is already gone, and the effect is one of blurring and confusion.

From the later poems we know that something went out of Clare's life in the years of enclosure, 1809–1820, but if we came on "Helpstone" in *Poems Descriptive of Rural Life and Scenery*, a more likely response would be simply that Clare laments because Goldsmith lamented. The volume, when it was published in 1820, was immediately popular. It was favorably reviewed and went into four printings in a year; in fact it sold more copies in its first year than any volume of Wordsworth's up to that time had ever sold. This shows how well the poems accorded with the public's expectations of what countryside poems should be, and how little Clare had as yet been able to say what had happened to him and to his place. Lacking a definitive text, one cannot say if the poems Taylor printed were exactly the poems Clare wrote, but as yet there was no strain between poet and editor-publisher because Clare was too excited to fuss. "Print just what suits you," he wrote Taylor, "and in any form whatever." However much the poems may have varied from standard literary English in grammar, spelling, punctuation, and diction, Clare clearly was aiming at standard English and therefore could welcome Taylor's help. He had already written drafts of hundreds of poems, and he knew he could write hundreds more, so of course Taylor could take whatever he liked and dress them as he saw fit.

Clare's feelings soon changed. At first he was thrilled that a London firm would publish his poems at all. When a well-meaning prospective patron, Lord Radstock, asked or told Clare to remove the ten lines in "Helpstone" about "accursed Wealth" because they were radical cant, they were removed, apparently without fuss. A second volume, *The Village Minstrel*, was rushed into print in 1821. It was no failure but it sold less well, and at the time Clare thought Taylor could have publicized it more, while Taylor was beginning to see only that the rage for poetry that had begun fifteen years earlier with Scott and Byron was ending. Both may have been right, but a note Clare wrote later shows there was more to it than that, for him at least:

> I began the Village Minstrel a long while before attempting to describe my own feelings and love for rural objects and I then began in good earnest with it after the trial of my first poems was made and compleated it was little time but I still was unsatisfied with it and am now and often feel sorry I did not withhold it a little longer for revision the reason why I dislike it is that it does not describe the feelings of a rhyming peasant strongly or localy enough

He was by then seeing *Poems Descriptive of Rural Life and Scenery* as the literary juvenilia it is. More was possible, but *The Village Minstrel* didn't "describe the feelings of a rhyming peasant strongly or localy enough," and Clare still had to keep on groping.

The story of *The Shepherd's Calendar*, which was mostly finished in 1823 but was not published until 1827 and then failed to gain much notice, is told in Clare's letters and in the Tibbles' standard biography of Clare. Clare was growing rebellious about the form his poems ought to take as he found a voice both stronger and more local; at the same time Taylor was convinced that Clare was getting more and more difficult, and that his poems were more than ever in need of editing and pruning if they were to enjoy any success. What neither the letters nor the biography shows is that in order to write more locally Clare had to write not just about Helpston as a distinct place, but about Helpston as though it had never been enclosed.

The quick early success, the gradual waning of that success, both contributed to Clare's seeing more clearly what poems he really wanted to write. Accompanying the success had been advice, most of it well enough meant but much of it misguided. Expunge radical cant. Expunge country terms and local dialect. Be less descriptive, be more reflective, offer more sentiment. Stay in your place. Stay clear of London. At one time or another Clare tried to follow all the advice, and presumably discovered he could not. The joy he felt in coming closer to being his own man and his own poet was accompanied by the bitter knowledge of the price he had to pay. "Stay in your place" proved a particularly painful matter. If it had simply meant "Stay in Helpston," that would have been easy enough, for Clare gave no sign of wanting to leave. The problem was different: what "place" did he have in Helpston?

After his first success, various friends and patrons put together an endowment of a few hundred pounds. This was invested and Clare received the income, which varied between forty and fifty pounds a year. His family was growing, and he almost always worked in the harvest in the summer. He made a little bit of money selling poems to magazines. Naively perhaps, he counted on income from his volumes of poetry and was embittered when sales were negligible. Accompanying the nagging money problem was another: his "place," his "class," was "rural poet," and he was the only one in it. He held on to his literary friends as best he could, but most of them were in London. The landed gentry around Helpston, the Fitzwilliams at Milton and the Marquis of Exeter at Burghley, could take kind notice of him, but he could neither be of their class nor, any longer, of the class of their servants. He had always been solitary and now became more so. Living mainly from a fund given him by patrons meant that, though he was in the society of rural laborers and his income was only slightly greater than theirs, he was not of this group; yet he had no other. He was, in addition, ill during most of the years before he moved to Northborough in 1832, although no clearer diagnosis was ever given him than that he suffered from undernourishment and mental strain. No wonder he was known mostly as a quiet shy man who became voluble when he drank; no wonder either that he drank too much and suffered afterward from great bouts of guilt.

In *Agrarian Age* Kenneth MacLean says with some disappointment that when Clare writes about the effects of enclosure on Helpston he seldom mentions the plight of the rural poor; he "has chosen to mourn the plumage and forget the dying bird." John Barrell responds to this, in his seminal book on Clare, by showing that while the laborers of Helpston were undoubtedly very poor, they may have been somewhat better off after enclosure than before. But as the passages quoted earlier from "The Flitting" and "Remembrances" show, it was the loss of the non-human life that most angered and saddened Clare. His eyes and ears were offended, more deeply than ours are when we see "Improvements, Ma'am!" where wood or field once were, but in a similar way. His response was not usually economic—how poor we have been made—or communal—the old way of life has gone—because he did not feel the effects of enclosure in his wallet and because in *The Shepherd's Calendar* and *The Midsummer Cushion*, as we will see, he was developing radical but mostly unlamenting ways of saying what had happened to the old life before enclosure.

His eye, I noted earlier, had always been kept low to the ground. In his essential solitude, he roamed Helpston parish and saw the effects of chopping, fencing, draining, and road-building on molehills, wildflowers, and low-nesting birds. This is the subject of the large and fully composed poems "Remembrances," "The Flitting," and "Decay." But it takes more than this sense of Clare as the poet lamenting in solitude to account for "Home

Pictures in May," which is really more characteristic of the strong local poet Clare made of himself, especially in *The Midsummer Cushion*:

> The sunshine bathes in clouds of many hues
> & mornings feet are gemed with early dews
> Warm daffodils about the garden beds
> Peep through their pale slim leaves their golden heads
> Sweet earthly suns of spring—the gossling broods
> In coats of sunny green about the road
> Waddle in extacy—& in rich moods
> The old hen leads her flickering chicks abroad
> Oft scuttling neath her wings to see the kite
> Hang wavering oer them in the springs blue light
> The sparrows round their new nests chirp with glee
> & sweet the robin springs young luxury shares
> Tutting its song in feathery gooseberry tree
> While watching worms the gardeners spade unbears

One might ask what makes this a poem at all rather than a hurriedly written series of impressions placed in lines that rhyme. Is it not notes for a poem Clare has not yet written?

The lack of internal grammar and of a consistent point of view are characteristics of the strong and local Clare. Some adjectives describe how something in the landscape is said to feel—the goslings "waddle in extacy" and the hen leads her chicks "in rich moods"—while others describe what Clare sees and hears—"flickering chicks," "feathery gooseberry tree," the robin "tutting its song." "We have the sense always," John Barrell writes, "that outside the poem are hundreds of images hammering to be admitted." Give Clare a title, a category of experience like "farmyard in May," and out tumbles as much of what he knows as can be crammed into fourteen lines. To be strong and local means *not* to have a prospect, a point of view, a landscape pictorially organized in the manner of Claude Lorrain and Thomson. In this way, Clare's method more closely resembles that of Constable, whose knowledge of his home scenes is like Clare's at Helpston, so secure as to need no explaining.

Clare has many poems in which he concentrates on one object

or one event for an entire poem without hurrying from object to object as he does in "Home Pictures in May." "The March Nightingale" and "The Thrushes Nest," for instance, look more like what other people call poems. The distinction, though, is clearly alien to Clare because in these poems too he is rushing to tell us all he knows. There is nothing scattered or inchoate about Clare's concentration on the farmyard at sunrise in "Home Pictures in May"; he needs no securer grammar than a list to convey his knowledge.

By itself "Home Pictures" has nothing to do with enclosures, but I did not mean to be obscure when I said that it would take more than knowing Clare as a lamenter of changes in his home landscape to understand this poem fully. Let me quote John Barrell here, writing about "The Pewits Nest," a poem similar in method to "Home Pictures in May": "Such clauses, almost always adjectival, do not suggest a sequence of separate observations through time—they offer instead a sense of place as a manifold of knowledge, recalled at once, necessarily written down bit by bit, but all simultaneously present in Clare's mind, so that the function of the syntax is not to *make* relations between different events, but to represent a pre-existent inseparability of all the events attached to the notion 'fallows in summer.'" And then, Barrell continues, not making as great a leap here as it might seem: "It may be that the particularly indivisible nature of what Clare knew about Helpston can be related to the mode of knowing available in an open-field landscape where, as we have seen, a great deal more was visible at once, at a glance, than in the more occluded landscape of enclosure." This observation applies to my point about Clare's vision: "Home Pictures in May" and most of the hundreds of Clare sonnets, though they may reveal little or nothing about whether their landscape is pre- or post-enclosure, have as their characteristic means of organization a pre-enclosure way of seeing and knowing.

The enclosers themselves were not eighteenth-century topographical poets, landscape painters, or aestheticians of the picturesque, but they too had an idea of how a place ought to look that could, first, be imposed on almost any landscape and, second, be compared to any other. Its aim is efficiency and order, its forms are squares and rectangles, differentiated and compartmentalized, so that part of the "beauty" of an enclosed landscape can only be seen from the sky. The visible markings are roads, ditches, and hedges, and places are shaped to fit prescribed activities and purposes.

By contrast, open field knowledge, pre-enclosure knowledge, has no such idea informing it. At some point in the past, in most cases before the end of the eleventh century, a parish and a village had been settled, and around the village fields were ploughed and pastures grown; at the edge of the cleared agricultural land there was commons or waste that continued until the next parish's fields began. Since the village was near the center of the parish and roads usually extended out from the village to the parish border like spokes on a wheel, pre-enclosure knowledge can be called circular, what the individual sees simply by standing in a place and turning around in a circle. The grammar of this knowledge is neither compartmentalized nor abstract, and it does not seek to interpret or to impose meaning or order. It is in this sense that poems like "Home Pictures in May" are pre-enclosure poems, and John Barrell's contribution was to relate Clare's poetic grammar to the grammar of his landscape.

We have now suggested three alien orders that were impinging on Clare: the order of standard literary English that Taylor imposed the more strongly the more determinedly Clare resisted it; the order of eighteenth-century literary landscapes that Clare had begun by imitating; the order of enclosed landscapes. For Clare, to resist one meant resisting the other two, and this should explain both the quality and the incidental nature of his attacks on enclosers and enclosures. He could lament the loss of heath, trees, and molehills in poems like "Remembrances," which are more composed in their demeanor than "Home Pictures in May." But if he was to resist successfully, he had to find a strong, local, pre-enclosure grammar, language, and scene, and the resistance would lead to celebration. I hope we are getting closer to being able to answer the question why the move to Northborough in 1832 elicited, among other things, deeply felt laments for a place and a boyhood lost fifteen to twenty years earlier.

In the stanza from "Remembrances" quoted earlier, Clare tells us about the changes on Langley bush, Cowper green, Spreading lea close, and Round oaks. All these places were southwest of Helpston village, in the part of the parish most affected by enclosure. The heath where Clare had gone out of his knowledge as a lad, the nearby pastures in which he and others had looked after sheep and cattle, were apparently Clare's favorite places. This land was cleared, ploughed, and hedged, and the remaining wood was dominated by gamekeepers who saw "trespasser" and "poacher" written on the brow of any who came near. The enclosing was finished by 1820, the year Clare's first volume was published. What, then, are we to make of "The Shepherd's Fire," which was written, as were most of Clare's greatest poems, between 1825 and 1832, as part of *The Midsummer Cushion*? When precisely is the action of the poem happening?

> On the rude heath yclad in furze & ling
> & oddling thorn that thick & prickly grows
> Shielding the shepherd when the rude wind blows
> & boys that sit right merry in a ring
> Round fires upon a molehill toasting sloes
> & crabs that froth & frizzle on the coals
> Loud is the gabble & the laughter loud
> The rabbits scarce dare peep from out their holes
> Unwont to mix with such a noisy crowd
> Some run to eke the fire—which many a cloud
> Of smoke curls up some on their haunches squat
> With mouth for bellows puffing till it flares
> Or if that fail one fans his napless hat
> & when the feast is done they squabble for their shares

A strong scene this, filled with local knowledge and language that inheres in a place, a place right there, nowhere else. The poem is not only composed in what Barrell describes as Clare's pre-enclosure syntax, but all the objects and activities here are indigenous to common-land grazing, and all would be greatly changed or disappear after enclosure: thorn, molehills, sloes, crabs, rabbits, and shepherd boys all were rooted out, drained out, or fenced out. Yet Clare offers "The Shepherd's Fire" in the present tense, all celebration, no lament, no nostalgia. To write the poem he has displaced himself a decade or more, and has done so without comment.

It is easy to imagine there must have been a struggle involved in this kind of displacement, and "Round Oak Spring," a poem we would have had to try to invent had Clare not written it, shows it taking place:

> Sweet brook Ive met thee many a summers day
> & ventured fearless in thy shallow flood
> & rambled oft thy sweet unwearied way
> Neath willows cool that on thy margin stood
> With crowds of partners in my artless play
> Grasshopper beetle bee & butterflye
> That frisked about as though in merye mood
> To see their old companion sporting bye
> Sweet brook lifes glories once were thine & mine
> Shades cloathed thy spring that now doth naked lie
> On thy white boiling sand the sweet woodbine
> Darkened & dipt its flowers—I mark & sigh
> & muse oer troubles since we met the last
> Like two fond friends whose happiness is past

"Remembrances" is a full-scale lament for lost worlds; "The Shepherd's Fire" is a full-scale celebration of a world we know was lost though the poem does not say so. "Round Oak Spring" should be placed between the two. It is a lament for a lost scene, but not the composed intoning of "Remembrances." Clare remembers the scene by the spring and rushes to it in his typical way: "Grasshopper beetle bee & butterflye." In the next lines he pulls back a little—"That frisked about as though in merye mood"—as if to acknowledge that he once unselfconsciously projected his mood onto the insects, and now must be more discreet and add "as though." "To see their old companion sporting bye" is eerie because it is hard to place in time; the insects see Clare as companion only back then, when he was a boy, yet "old companion" seems to say either "dear old Clare" as a term of familiarity or to pull the companion back into a time closer to the time of the poem's composition. This leads him to his one description of Round Oak spring at present, after drainage—"that now doth naked lie / On thy white boiling sand"—but the sight is too painful and he flees back to the past—"the sweet woodbine / Darkened & dipt its flowers." But in a poem that shifts like this, Clare cannot stay there, and so he now marks and sighs and muses on the troubles of the spring and himself since they first were companions.

Clare discovered how to be a strong and local peasant rhymer, but to do this he had to deceive his eyes and ears because his way of being strong and local was to celebrate a world that was no longer there. If Clare retreated into the past, it was not in defeat but in a struggle against the alien orders imposed by enclosers, editors, and the landscape poetry of his youth. That is what I meant by calling these struggles a refiner's fire for Clare. With "Round Oak Spring" in mind, we can sense how much pain underlies "Home Pictures in May" and "The Shepherd's Fire," themselves poems totally free of pain. Clare had to punish himself, to trap himself between "I see" and "I saw," in order to write the celebrating poems that are his most distinctive achievements.

I want now to stalk John Barrell in some of his most trenchant pages about Clare; my aim is some different emphases and conclusions, first about *The Shepherd's Calendar*, which Barrell calls Clare's best long poem, and second about Clare's place in the literature of the period. Leading up to his discussion of *The Shepherd's Calendar*, Barrell quotes the "Sonnet to——," which begins:

> I walked with poesy in the sonnets bounds
> With little hopes yet many a wild delight
> As timid children take their summer rounds
> & scarce dare leave their cottage out of sight

"The form of the sonnet," Barrell writes, "is identified with the 'bounds' of a landscape, and it restricts him . . . to his 'knowledge,' as children are restricted to the area around their cottage."

As the poem proceeds, Clare imagines himself straying from these boundaries:

> Skimmed like a bird and found no resting place
> Heaths flat & sky its undivided blue
> A timid minstrel through their varied maze

There is a world out there, beyond Clare's bounds, and it is in the same direction, southwest over Emmonsailes Heath, that he went out of his knowledge as a boy. When he imagines going out there, he is imagining an alien action in an alien place, skimming like a bird and finding no resting place, and becoming thereby a timid minstrel.

Helpston was bondage for Clare, but within these confines he found "the sonnets bounds," which enabled him to write his strong local peasant poetry. He knew perfectly well what lay out there: the lime kiln, Martha Turner's childhood home, Milton manor, the Burghley estate, the road to London he had been on half a dozen times. He also knew that in "the little sonnets garden home" he had found himself as a poet, no matter how trapped and time-warped the place had made him. He could move out of Helpston but he could not be a poet out of Helpston, though the anguish involved in being a poet there might well make him want to leave. The bonding of the parish to the sonnet could also tempt him toward the long poem, and that, I think, was sheer delusion, a temptation suggested by the metaphor more than by anything he might seriously hope to find in the long poem, or in the long journey either. If in breaking out of Helpston he becomes "a timid minstrel," he might have anticipated that something similar would happen if he broke very far out of "the sonnets bounds."

The long poem in question is *The Shepherd's Calendar*, the volume that followed *The Village Minstrel* and the first in which Clare's distinctive syntax and local voice are present, in which the eager alertness of seeing and knowing sets him apart from his more sedate and measured predecessors. There are, unquestionably, splendid passages in *The Shepherd's Calendar*, though most are like the quick bursts of the shorter poems. The feeling that outside the poem hundreds of images are battering to get in is replaced by the feeling that the images are indeed in, and tending to swamp each other. The wonderful feeling that objects and events are all simultaneous, the hallmark of all Clare's best poetry, is harder and harder to convey the longer the poem becomes. The freedom of the form gives Clare what his description of the world outside Helpston in "Sonnet to——" promised him: no resting place.

"For Clare," Barrell says, "a place is a good deal more than a landscape, a place is a manifold of images, not of visual images only, and not only of topography but of the people and living things that work in the place." Quite true, but the statement blurs the role played by people and their work in Clare's poetry. *The Shepherd's Calendar* is written in Clare's pre-enclosure manner, and is indeed about "the people and the living things that work in the place," but Clare's solitariness as a child, and his isolation in the one-person class "rural poet," kept him further from adult laboring life than he perhaps realized. Certainly he knew more about that life than other poets or all but a few of the literate people in England, and this must have made the idea of writing a new calendar especially appealing. Crabbe, for instance, was still a popular poet; his *Tales from the Hall* in 1819 had been given the kind of advance against royalties usually reserved for Byron or Tom Moore, and for Clare Crabbe was a mere parson poet: "Whats he know of the distresses of the poor musing over a snug coal fire in his parsonage box." As for Wordsworth, Clare wrote an imitation "in ridicule of his affectations of simplicity." Clare admired Keats, but Keats was city-bred and his countryside was all nymphs and dryads. A calendar was perfect because no one knew rural seasons as Clare knew them.

In a poem as long as *The Shepherd's Calendar* it would be easy to show, as I have alleged, Clare being a little too far removed from the people who live and work in the countryside and equally easy to show Clare intimately expressing that working and living. Best, then, to quote from the latter, and to show what seems limiting or mistaken even when Clare is giving us what other poets could not:

The haytime butterflyes dance up and down
And gads that teaze like whasps the timid maid
And drive the herdboys cows to pond and shade
Who when his gods assistance fails to stop
Is forcd his half made oaten pipes to drop
And start and halloo thro the dancing heat
To keep their gadding tumult from the wheat
Who in their rage will dangers overlook
And leap like hunters oer the pasture brook
Brushing thro blossomd beans in maddening haste
And 'stroying corn they scarce can stop to taste
Labour pursues its toil in weary mood
And feign would rest wi shadows in the wood
The mowing gangs bend oer the beeded grass
Where oft the gipseys hungry journeying ass
Will turn its wishes from the meadow paths
Listning the rustle of the falling swaths

This is about the length of a sonnet; it is from "June," and seems to me good, especially the lines about the cows getting in the corn. I hope I have chosen fairly.

More than once Clare complained that gypsies were among the victims of enclosure; either because of or in spite of their being liars and thieves, they were among the attractive parts of his childhood world. The presence of the gypsy's ass thus identifies this as a pre-enclosure world, but we hardly need the detail. The whole thing is a child's vision: the herdboys, the cows, and the dogs are in the foreground, while the adults are over there, and called "labour" and "the mowing gangs." This remains true even in the fine passage about the plowman that follows immediately:

The ploughman sweats along the fallow vales
And down the suncrackt furrow slowly trails
Oft seeking when a thirst the brooks supply
Where brushing eager the brinks bushes bye
For coolest water he oft brakes the rest
Of ring dove brooding oer its idle nest
And there as loath to leave the swaily place

Though Clare was that plowman at one time or another, what he describes here is strictly a figure seen from the outside, in a landscape, and seen as a child would see: a man getting thirsty, going to the brook, drinking, disturbing the ring dove.

When one does not try to read *The Shepherd's Calendar* as a long poem, or even as twelve long poems, but as something like a sonnet sequence, the poetry seems very good, near the level of Clare's shorter poems. Yet Clare is always, I feel, paying the penalty for celebrating, for being forced to celebrate, a Helpston he was cut off from and could express only as something seen by a child. It is not that the child did not see enough, as there is material for four thousand lines, but it is all the same kind of seeing, and is bound to be better on weather, ground, birds, and insects, Clare's childhood companions in truth, than on the laboring people. Barrell notes the objection that Clare's people are not individual characters and rightly replies: "The people Clare writes about are what they do; if they were anything else— if they had, somehow, *more* character—then the sense of place they help create in Clare's poems would change, and would have engaged in some compromise with what it is designed to ex- clude—the spirit and values of agrarian capitalism." There is no point in complaining that Clare's human figures are one-dimen- sional, unlike people in Crabbe's tales or the *Lyrical Ballads*. But as Clare's characters are always seen externally, we learn too little about what it is they do. We learn little about sex, except as youthful courtship, about drink, about illness, about infant deaths and old age, about what, in the usual sense, it means to be poor. The child's vision could not bring these in, and much of the strength of the impoverished people is thereby excluded. The despised Crabbe, most of whose characters are only types, could bring into his tales facts and qualities about his people that Clare, who presumably knew more, could not.

I have tried to describe Clare's situation so as to indicate his limitations even when he was writing at or close to his best. It was an extraordinary set of circumstances he confronted, and his response was not only poetry of a very high order, but poetry written with courage and punishing determination. In the years he spent in asylums he often became confused about who he was, but I hope I have shown how the process began years earlier. In learning to say, and in a way no one before him had done, *where* he was he effectively put himself in danger of losing touch with *when* he was. On this reckoning, it is not at all surprising that in his forties he began to write about his first love, Mary Joyce, confusing her with his wife, and confusing events and feelings of thirty years before with those of the present.

Barrell's final placing of Clare, and of his relation to us, is as follows: "The eighteenth-century poets, compared with Clare, moved as tourists through the places they wrote about—but we are all tourists now, so that insofar as Clare was successful in expressing his own sense of place, he was writing himself out of the mainstream of European literature." We know the last statement is true. Clare's greatest book, *The Midsummer Cushion*, carefully transcribed by Clare himself, was known by 1893, during a Clare Centenary, to exist in the Peterborough Museum. No one published anything from it until Edmund Blunden did in 1920, and it was not published, as I noted earlier, until 1978, when it got scant notice for such an important event. The *Norton Anthology of English Literature*, which in America has something of the status of the Oxford anthologies, prints nothing from it, and prints the few late lyrics it includes as though John Taylor had been right all along in cleaning up Clare's texts to make them more readable. But for all this I am not convinced that the relation of literature to place, and to the study of the literature of places, is, or needs to be, as fixed as Barrell implies.

Before I went there, I knew I had no chance of seeing pre-enclosure Helpston; what bits of that remain, like Clare's cottage, the Blue Boar, the church, the old vicarage, are only items to the visitor, not parts of a world, and even those who live in Helpston, who do see them as parts of a world, cannot see them as parts of the Helpston of 1800. But the current visitor is lucky in one respect. Helpston parish's one piece of rising ground, Emmonsailes Heath, which was enclosed and plowed, has now gone back to rough woodland, though a rebarbative conifer forest now keeps one from seeing this from the village. One can, though, walk to the heath and imagine the lad walking out of his knowledge. Such a walk reminded me how much even a small rise in ground can mean in otherwise flat terrain, especially when it leads out of plowed field to heath, as it did for Clare as a lad. It was easier to see then why Northborough, only three miles away but tabletop flat and on the edge of a large fen, could be a place that triggered those poems about how far Clare had come from those spots his heart esteemed—how far in space, but especially in time. It also seemed easier to wonder *when* Clare was during his adult years in Helpston, before the move, while writing his greatest poems.

The one Clare poem I fully expected to "see" was indeed there to be seen. From Helpston the distance to Glinton's church spire in the neighboring parish is just under two miles:

> Glinton thy taper spire predominates
> Over the level landscape—& the mind
> Musing—the pleasing picture contemplates
> Like elegance of beauty much refined
> By taste—that almost deifys and elevates
> Ones admiration making common things
> Around it glow with beautys not their own
> Thus all around the earth superior springs
> Those straggling trees though lonely seem not lone
> But in thy presence wear superior power
> & een each mossed and melancholly stone
> Gleaning cold memories round oblivions tower
> Seem types of fair eternity—& hire
> A lease from fame by thy enchanting spire

This is a "scene," and Clare begins as any topographical poet might do. As he muses, though, he moves unselfconsciously from moral to aesthetic to religious language, so that what is "a pleasing picture" can "almost deify" and "elevates / Ones admiration," and does both these at once. What I had not seen until I actually saw the spire, and standing in Helpston, was something for which the evidence is clear in the poem itself, namely, that even here, in a poem that seems to find Clare standing and looking from a single spot, there is no fixed point of view. To see the spire predominate is to stand away from it, even as far as Helpston. To see straggling trees wearing the spire's superior power is to stand much closer, and to see mossed and melancholy stones—of the church, or of the gravestones—is to be much closer still. His being able to be in a number of places at once, presenting as one experience what must necessarily be a number of experiences, helps explain his casual mixing of his words of wonder and praise, moral, aesthetic, religious. It is not one of Clare's best poems, but it is good enough to show how he made his best poems strong, local, original. It was in groping to figure out where Clare was standing to see Glinton spire that I realized, with that sense of prior knowledge made active, that of course he was not standing in one place at all.

Clare's is a special case because his world, by choice and by imagining, was extremely localized, even more so than Jane Austen's. As a result, his departure from the poetry of more generalized landscape on which he was raised had to be radical, especially given the dislocations brought about by the enclosures. He was among the first who were forced, as part of the process of being or becoming a writer at all, to make a particular place matter. In this respect it is Austen, of all the figures in this book, whom he most resembles, because in moving from the generalized landscapes they had read about, and from the generalized landscapes of their own juvenilia, they moved toward a sense of particularized place that is not to be generalized about. Austen's great sentence about a mind lively and at ease is as true of Clare as of her. The terrible thing about Clare's experience is that in order thus to be lively and at ease in his poems he had to twist himself out of time and move toward madness.

But his way of lamenting, and especially his way of celebrating, put a place, and a kind of poetry, on the map that without him would never have found a voice. He altered, and he continues to be able to alter, our sense of what a place is, and of what a poem is as well. As to whose sense actually is altered, since we are all tourists now and since Clare has yet to make his true mark on the world, it can be said that if we are tourists we are also historians, moving back in time as well as around in space, knowing that even the best of us do both kinds of moving somewhat clumsily. Our sense of tradition, we know, is something we must consciously construct as historians. But, forced to do this, we can see Clare as clearly as anyone else of his time, and we can thus see how wasteful it is to define the "mainstream" of the literature of this period in such a way that Clare is written out of it, "a third-generation Romantic" or some such. John Barrell showed that we could, in effect, alter the course of that stream by careful reconstruction and reconsideration of materials, many of them long familiar.

But the great creator of the Romantic mainstream, as it is usually described and defined, is Wordsworth, and it is to him we must now turn.

# VI

### ❧ WILLIAM WORDSWORTH

FOR FIFTY YEARS Wordsworth's homes were at Grasmere and Rydal, which are almost in the middle of a triangle that has as its points Cockermouth, his birthplace, Hawkshead, his school, and Penrith, home of his mother's family and his vacation home after his father's death. No place inside this triangle is more than thirty miles from any other. Until he went to Cambridge Wordsworth had not left the area, and in his last fifty years to leave it was to travel, to be abroad. The association of Wordsworth with the heart of the Lake District is as complete, and justly famous, as that of the Brontë sisters with Haworth.

The association tends to hide a tale, however, one that the essayist of place can delight in telling. It deals much with quite familiar materials, but also with some that have come into prominence only in the last decade or so. One reason it has not been told before is that Wordsworth's insistence on arranging his poems by categories rather than by dates has made it difficult to read him chronologically; another is that the chronology is so very famous in its general outlines that it has not usually seemed necessary to do more than divide his career into two periods, the great and the late, and then only to debate the dividing line between the two. Stephen Gill, when he edited Wordsworth for the Oxford Authors series in 1984, could claim that "Here for the first time a selection of Wordsworth's work is offered in which the poems are ordered according to the date of their composition, and presented in texts which give as nearly

as possible their earliest completed state." And Jonathan Wordsworth, in 1982, felt obliged to say what no one would have had
to say had the subject been Milton, or Blake, or Keats: "Some
may feel that I emphasize too frequently the dates and facts of
composition, but the circumstances in which the poetry was
written altered very much during Wordsworth's most creative
years, and only a sharp sense of chronology can enable one to
isolate the qualities of mind and art that stay the same." Both
Gill and Jonathan Wordsworth have contributed to, and relied
upon, the publication of the 1799 two-part *Prelude* in 1977, and
have drawn on the Cornell Wordsworth editions of "The Ruined
Cottage" and "Home at Grasmere," which show the evolution
of important parts of *The Recluse*. There is no question but that
some of the most important details of Wordsworth's work in the
crucial decade of 1795–1805 are now much easier to see than
they were a generation ago.

But it has been possible to see all along that the lifetime
association of Wordsworth with the Lake District was not destined from the outset. After he left Hawkshead School in 1787,
and especially after he left Cambridge in 1790, Wordsworth was
only briefly in Cumberland and Westmoreland. His family had
long since broken up, his friends were elsewhere, and his incli-
nation for many of these years took him to the Continent. He
and his sister, Dorothy, were reunited at Windy Brow, near Keswick, in 1794, but after he nursed the dying Raisley Calvert
there and received Calvert's legacy, which left him free to live
where he pleased, he went to Dorset, then Somerset, then Germany.

When William and Dorothy returned from Germany in the
spring of 1799, they settled briefly in County Durham, at Sockburn on Tees, the home of the Hutchinsons, friends of their
youth. From there Wordsworth wrote his friend and publisher,
Joseph Cottle, that "We have not as yet determined where we
shall settle; we have no particular house in view." At the same
time, Dorothy wrote: "I think Racedown [in Dorset] is the place
dearest to my recollection on the whole surface of the island."
Having been unpleasantly far from books in Germany, being near
a library was a consideration, but more important was being near

Coleridge. The Wordsworths had twice moved to be near him, first to Alfoxden in Somerset, then to Germany. It may have been little more than Thomas Poole's inability to find a house suitable for the Coleridges in Nether Stowey that inclined Coleridge back toward London, and his decision in turn may have inclined Wordsworth to look elsewhere. But, in any event, had he and Dorothy gone back to Dorset, or to Somerset, there would have been little reason for anyone outside family and friends to associate Wordsworth with the Lakes at all during his lifetime.

Indeed, had the Hutchinsons not lived in the north of England, Wordsworth might never have proposed to Coleridge that they take a walking trip in the Lake District in the fall of 1799. But after Coleridge rushed to Sockburn upon hearing that Wordsworth was ill, it seemed appropriate to show him the places of Wordsworth's youth. The two were joined for part of their trip by Wordsworth's brother John, and after the three had spent some days in and around Grasmere, Wordsworth wrote Dorothy: "You will think my plan a mad one but I have thought of building a house there by the lake side." Later he was to describe how as a boy he had thought, upon passing through Grasmere, that he would love to live there, and he remembered how much he and Dorothy had loved walking there in 1794. Still, in November of 1799 to think of moving there might well seem a mad idea to Dorothy. Nothing ever did come of building a house, but soon William was negotiating to rent a cottage at Town End—Dove Cottage, as it was to be called later. By Christmas he had returned to Sockburn to pick up Dorothy and their belongings and the two had begun to settle in, far from Coleridge, far from any library, far from friends. The most Wordsworth could claim then of their chosen home was that it was indeed a fine place in which to write a poem to be called *The Recluse*.

He was not, in his own eyes, going "home." A few months later, having seen Wordsworth at Town End, Coleridge wrote: "He will never quit the north of England. His habits are more assimilated with the habits there; there he and his sister are exceedingly beloved, enthusiastically. Such differences do small sympathies make, such as voice, pronunciation, etc." But Wordsworth did not see himself as going "home"; in the 1800 section of the almost inarticulately ecstatic "Home at Grasmere," he imagines he has arrived, not at home but in Eden, where there is "A blended holiness of earth and sky," "And now 'tis mine for life!" Yet when he notes that two swans who had moved to Grasmere that winter could not be seen in the spring, he says he and Dorothy were especially drawn to the swans because

> . . . their state so much resembled ours,
> They also having chosen this abode;
> They strangers, and we strangers; they a pair
> And we a solitary pair like them.

Indeed, in a passage of the poem that may not have been written before 1806, Wordsworth refers to himself as "Newcomer though I be."

Wordsworth wrote twenty poems in his first year in Grasmere, and eighteen are explicitly about places in and around Grasmere. In all of them there are signs of his feeling like a thrilled newcomer—not someone to whom this area is familiar from childhood but rather one who is not a tourist because he has come to stay. Nothing that he or Dorothy wrote in that first happy year, in letter, journal, or verse, indicates that they thought about or visited any of the places of their childhood; in the heart of the triangle, they did not acknowledge that the triangle existed.

This might well strike anyone as odd, but what makes it odder still is that Wordsworth had spent much of the previous winter of 1798–99, in Germany, writing about his childhood, to all intents and purposes inventing childhood in literature, memorializing it in poetry that is riveted in its home places. So there are two Wordsworths, two ways of living in and writing about the mountains and lakes of his "home." I hope to show that the trip to Germany and the subsequent move to Grasmere were a watershed in Wordsworth's career.

"If the first *Recluse* poems owe much of their existence to Coleridge's presence in 1797–98, the first *Prelude* poetry owes its existence to Coleridge's absence from Wordsworth in 1798–99." Thus Kenneth Johnston begins his reconstruction of the relation between *The Recluse,* the philosophical poem on "Man, Nature, and Society" that Coleridge insisted he write, and the untitled *Prelude,* somewhat ironically called informally "the poem to Coleridge." By the first *Recluse* poems Johnston means the story of Margaret ("The Ruined Cottage"), the encounter with the discharged soldier (eventually *The Prelude,* IV, 362–504), "The Old Cumberland Beggar," and "Night Piece," poems mostly describing people in extreme states of poverty and misery and trying to ask how we are best to respond to them.

Johnston does not quite say that *The Prelude* would not have been written had the Wordsworths not parted from Coleridge in Germany in the autumn of 1798, a parting that seems the result of impersonal considerations to do with money and with being in situations where German had to be spoken. But he rightly wants to highlight the stress of Wordsworth's finding himself, in the last and coldest winter of the eighteenth century, in a provincial German town, with limited funds, limited knowledge of German, no library, no friends, and no Coleridge. "Wordsworth found himself," he says, "in the sort of enforced exile that has stimulated many writers, from Ovid to Joyce, to creative self-preservation." But that hardly explains why he not only turned inward to preserve himself, but, crucially, turned to the self he was as a child.

"Tintern Abbey" provided some impetus. It had been written the previous summer and inserted in *Lyrical Ballads* just as the volume was going to press; it offers Wordsworth's first statement about his adult self in relation to his childhood, and it stands apart from the rest of the *Lyrical Ballads,* in no way participating in their experiments in subject and diction. Its subject is not of course childhood as such, but a contrast between two visits to the Wye valley, in 1793 and 1798, with the memory of the first visit feeding Wordsworth in the years between. In 1793 he was "like a roe":

> I bounded o'er the mountains, by the sides
> Of the deep rivers, and the lonely streams,
> Wherever nature led; more like a man
> Flying from something that he dreads, than one
> Who sought the thing he loved.

117

In 1798 he hears the "still, sad music of humanity" as he looks on the scene and feels "A presence that disturbs me with the joy / Of elevated thoughts." By comparison, then, the Wordsworth of 1793 seems so much like the Wordsworth of his boyhood that both can be placed under the mantle of "the hour/Of thoughtless youth" and the boyhood itself can be enclosed in a parenthesis:

> For nature then
> (The coarser pleasures of my boyish days,
> And their glad animal movements all gone by)
> To me was all in all.

But if such references to his childhood were adequate for the purposes of "Tintern Abbey," they clearly were not sufficient. His relation to nature, to the powers he felt at work there, and to his experiences with those powers, all were distorted in "Tintern Abbey."

Before this, childhood had never seemed important enough to warrant more than passing reference or a summary like the one in "Tintern Abbey." The famous Rousseau in his famous *Confessions* has some pages on his early years, but he unblushingly describes his childhood as though it happened so that he could make a point about it. Wordsworth marks the real change. The reference to "The coarser pleasures of my boyish days" in "Tintern Abbey" is like one an earlier writer might have made; the repeated "Was it for this?" that haunts the opening of the 1799 *Prelude* shows him beginning to take seriously what happened in the years between infancy and young adulthood.

Coleridge's role here is largely negative; his absence left a void. From 1795 to 1798 Coleridge seems the dominant one of the two, or the three. Neither man had produced the work he hoped to do, but Coleridge was fuller of ambitions, ideas, possibilities. It was the Wordsworths who moved from Racedown to Alfoxden in 1797; by 1800 the roles had reversed and Coleridge took Greta Hall in Keswick to be near the Wordsworths. The fact that Coleridge had many reasons for going to Germany in 1798 and the Wordsworths went only because Coleridge was going says something about the state of their relations then. When Cole-

ridge went to Ratzeburg and the Wordsworths to Goslar, he
assumed Wordsworth would plunge back into writing *The Recluse*. Coleridge's own epic work might, as he conceived it,
require a decade of reading before writing could begin, but all
Wordsworth needed, so they both seem to have thought, was to
be a recluse.

In Goslar Wordsworth wrote the first of the two parts of the
1799 *Prelude*, "Nutting," "There was a boy," four of the Lucy
poems, and eight poems about the old master at Hawkshead
School he called "Matthew." Given this production, the repeated
"Was it for this?" serves as both apology and explanation for his
not continuing *The Recluse*, as if he were saying, "I was born
and raised to fulfill a high purpose like *The Recluse*, and I am
sorry I am not fulfilling it; back then, in my childhood, is the
source of a power that compels me to make it, and myself then,
the subject of my poetry." *Recluse* subjects might still be his
subjects, but they had to be put at a greater distance. There is a
long study yet to be done of Wordsworth's Goslar poetry seen as
perhaps his greatest creative period; here I can confine myself
to the material that went into the 1799 *Prelude*. From Part I,
and the notebooks that underlie it, two startling facts emerge.
First, in the months in Goslar Wordsworth wrote all the major
childhood episodes—bathing in the Derwent; skating; stealing
the raven's eggs, the boat, and the trapped birds; the Winander
boy; the drowned man; beneath Penrith beacon; waiting for the
horses—and these were almost all the episodes of childhood he
would *ever* write. Second, the "large" statements, the generalizations, the philosophy, are all here too, which shows that from
the beginning *The Prelude* was a kind of alternative to *The
Recluse*, though Wordsworth did not know this and would have
denied it. Eventually, it was able to crowd out *The Recluse* so
that that poem did not have to be finished.

Here is the end of the description of visiting the raven's nest,
as found in the earliest, the JJ, notebook:

> While on the perilous edge I hung alone
> With what strange utterance did the loud dry wind
> Blow through my ears the sky seemd not a sky

Of earth, and with what motion moved the clouds
Ah not in vain ye beings of the hills
And ye that walk the woods and open heaths
By moon or starlight thus from my first day
Of childhood did ye love to interweave
The passions [                              ]
Not with the mean & vullgar works of man
But with high objects with eternal things
With life & nature, purifying thus
The elements of feiling & of thought
And sanctifying by such disc[i]pline
Both pain & fear untill we recognize
A grandeur in the beatings of the heart.

Of the sixteen lines above, the first four and the last seven were preserved word for word down through the 1850 *Prelude*; "ye beings of the hills" is taken from here and reappears as "Ye visions of the hills" in the apostrophe after the skating scene; most of the middle lines were placed, in slight altered form, following "Wisdom and Spirit of the Universe!" after the stolen boat. So units, once written, were never discarded, though they could be moved around and lines, often long passages, could be added.

One cannot dwell too much on the trust that Wordsworth reveals. Whatever he thought he was doing when first writing the JJ Notebook he subsequently trusted himself to have done. We can see this in three different ways. First, Wordsworth decided in 1798–99 what incidents from his childhood he wanted, and how much weight and prominence he wanted to give each one. If we include the meeting with the discharged soldier, "There was a boy," and "Nutting," which are not in the 1799 *Prelude* but were written by the time Part I was finished, everything Wordsworth was ever to feel he needed from his childhood was written in the space of a few months. In most cases that includes the narratives and the generalizing statements about what he had experienced and what, residually, those experiences had yielded.

Second, in these generalizing passages Wordsworth names the powers he encountered as "Ye beings of the hills," "Ye powers of earth! ye Genii of the springs," and so on. There is no sign that he wanted to restrict these powers to local deities, but clearly and persistently he speaks of them as being expressed *there*, in a place, in the woods, in the water, on the crags. We might place these passages along a chronological continuum, putting before them, say, the more pantheistic suggestion of "something far more deeply interfused" in "Tintern Abbey," as against "the mind of Man, / My haunt, and the main region of my song" of the preamble to *The Recluse*. If we were to talk about Wordsworth's thinking, his conception of powers internal and powers external and their relations to each other, we would then seem committed to reconciling the disparate elements along this continuum or else to showing how Wordsworth "changed his mind."

The textual evidence shows something about Wordsworth's trust that may obviate the need for such inquiry. We know that between 1799 and 1805 Wordsworth "changed his mind," and we can see it in the Intimations Ode, in the revisions and additions that went into the 1805 *Prelude*, in the "Ode to Duty" and the "Elegiac Stanzas." In none of these poems and passages does Wordsworth have the beings of the hills and the powers of the earth and sky doing the things they did in the 1799 *Prelude*: disciplining, peopling the mind, intertwining, impressing, using severe interventions. But whenever he returned to *The Prelude*, regardless of what he then thought about the relation of self to external power, he repeated what he had said in 1799, even though in some cases he was contradicting what he was saying in parts of *The Prelude* written later. He is trusting the boyhood experience to have revealed the presence of these powers, and he is trusting himself in 1798–99 to have named and described them rightly.

Third, there is the remarkable fact of Wordsworth's trusting his original wording and phrasing throughout his work on *The Prelude* over forty years. It is quite true that the fun in comparing different versions of a text is to note differences—my favorite passage in Geoffrey Hartman's *Wordsworth's Poetry*, for instance, is his work with six versions of a few lines in Book VI where each small change shows a shift in thought or feeling. But

here are the key lines about the nighttime stealing from bird
traps in the JJ Notebook:

>                       Sometimes strong desire
> Resistless over came me & the bird
> Th[at] was the captive of another's toils
> Became my prey, and then [          ] I heard
> Low breathings coming after me and sounds
> Of undistinguishable motion steps
> Almost as silent as the turf they trod.

There are some phrases we might call "missing," meaning they
are not here but are in the 1805 and 1850 versions—"among the
solitary hills," "O'erpowered my better reason," "and when the
deed was done." All these are in the V manuscript of some
months later in 1799 and none alters the meaning of the passage
more than very slightly. One reason it is difficult to read the
1799 *Prelude* as an independent poem is that for long stretches
it so closely resembles the 1805 or 1850 *Prelude* we know.

In case I have not yet made it clear, it was not so much the
boy's experience as the 1799 poet's writing that the later Wordsworth trusted. He was willing to make some little alterations in
"what happened," so that he might have been carousing or walking alone before he met the discharged soldier, and he might
have seen the murderer's name or the outline of his grave in the
episode beneath Penrith beacon. But for the most part, if the
1799 poet said that something was so, he was presumed to have
had the right relation with the childhood experience; he knew
he had said it right.

For a number of reasons, I do not sense that Wordsworth in
*The Prelude* committed himself to place in any special way. The
generalizing passages, which not only were present in the earliest
versions but sometimes exist in the notebooks without any at-
taching particulars, suggest that while, yes, this did happen in a
particular time and place, at another time and place the same
power could be at work in the same or similar ways. This is
why in revising Wordsworth can shift his generalizing passages
around to follow different episodes. Nor is he, as Hartman has
suggested, responding to a particular *genius loci*. "Consult the

Genius of the place in all," says Pope, offering advice to someone making a house or garden, in control of the land; little could be further from Wordsworth in these scenes. The boy is an intruder, knowing nothing of the genius of the place, but made receptive, usually by fear, to the power when it is expressed there. Because Wordsworth gives us something closer to dream landscape than to Thomsonian description, unless we know where the events actually happened we cannot easily find these childhood scenes. We know he lived among hills, mountains, rivers, waterfalls, lakes, sheep, and shepherds, because these are mentioned and praised for helping his nurture and discipline. But Wordsworth's trust in his experience works against his feeling the need to give us coordinates or to help make us part of the scene ourselves. It is not surprising that Wordsworthians took a long time deciding where Wordsworth was when he stole the boat or waited for the horses, and these are among the more fully specified episodes.

The outstanding instances of Wordsworth's trust are the two famous "spots of time": the scene below Penrith beacon and the waiting for the horses outside Hawkshead. In form they are not much different from the other boyhood scenes, but from the beginning they were set apart. The episodes were written some months after the others, and in the 1799 *Prelude* they are separated from the other charged experiences by a hundred lines of description of uncharged card playing, fishing, and kite flying; they are not accounted for in the poem by any intervention of the beings of the hills or the spirits of the sky, and are among the most enigmatic passages in a poem full of enigmas, in part because Wordsworth does not really attempt to explain them. In the scenes from Part I of 1799 that went into Book I in 1805 and 1850 we do not feel any pressing need for explanation; it is not difficult to say what happened in the incidents or what happens in the verse. When Empson says that "Wordsworth frankly had no inspiration other than his use, when a boy, of the mountains as a totem, or father-substitute," we may feel that he is or is not "right," but we are sure the mountain episodes do not require such determined interpretation. The spots of time are different. There has been much excellent work on them, most recently by Johnston, Jonathan Wordsworth, and especially David Ellis in

*Wordsworth, Freud, and the Spots of Time,* but even as these passages become clearer they remain—one wants to say *therefore* they remain—enigmas.

Starting with Wordsworth's statement that the spots of time show that the mind is "lord and master," while "outward sense / Is but the obedient servant of her will," David Ellis points out that the two episodes are quite different from each other in this regard. In the first scene the outward sense, as it sees the pool, the woman, and the beacon, seems to dictate to the mind what the experience is to be, while in the second the mind is able to make outward sense obedient to its will: Wordsworth's feeling about his father's death is projected onto the experience of waiting for the horses before he died, and his memory of the incident is recorded somewhat differently from the way he says it happened. I think this difference between the two spots is not critical. In the scene below Penrith beacon the crucial fact is that Wordsworth takes the "ordinary sight" of pool, woman, and beacon and paints it with "visionary dreariness," thus controlling what the outward sense insists on. But, as often happens with these passages, becoming clear about one thing helps point up what remains obscure. What did the boy see while looking at the murderer's grave or name that made him flee, that helped create the visionary dreariness? Is the loss of the servant central or incidental to the experience? Why did Wordsworth place, or displace, his father's death onto the scene of his waiting for the horses? What difference does it make that in this passage his two descriptions of the event are not quite the same? What is it that allows these scenes of bleakness and horror to yield a fructifying and restoring virtue?

To go to Penrith and Hawkshead to compare scene with poem yields further puzzles. One might have thought that one reason Jonathan Wordsworth calls these border experiences is that they take place at the border between settled land and wilderness. Not so. The hill outside Penrith is, or was, bare enough, but it is so close to the town as to make it difficult to feel lost there, even allowing for the boy's facing away from town as he flees the grave and climbs the hill. In this case one can say that he was only five or six when it happened and assume that that accounts for the discrepancy between the scene in the poem and the scene in fact. In the other scene, though, Wordsworth is thirteen, yet one goes to Hawkshead expecting border country and finds instead a pleasant, even pretty landscape, one that cannot yield "a crag, an eminence" for him to have climbed to look for the horses. (As I will have occasion to make more of, Grasmere, by comparison with Hawkshead, can be quite wild and bleak, yet Wordsworth describes it in terms suggesting golden, glowing peacefulness.) Here Wordsworth's mind is so much lord and master that a mere observer finds it difficult to imagine these experiences in those places.

But this does not negate the relevance of place; quite the opposite:

> The day before the holidays began,
> Feverish, and tired and restless, I went forth
> Into the fields, impatient for the sight
> Of those three horses which should bear us home,
> My Brothers and myself. There was a crag,
> An eminence which from the meeting point
> Of two highways ascending overlooked
> At least a long half-mile of those two roads,
> By each of which the expected steeds might come,
> The choice uncertain. Thither I repaired
> Up to the highest summit; 'twas a day
> Stormy, and rough, and wild, and on the grass
> I sate, half-sheltered by a naked wall;
> Upon my right hand was a single sheep,
> A whistling hawthorn on my left, and there,
> Those two companions at my side, I watched
> With eyes intensely straining as the mist
> Gave intermitting prospect of the wood
> And plain beneath.

It is, like the first spot of time, "in truth, an ordinary sight," and Wordsworth works to keep his language flat and uncharged, so that those who stare at these lines can feel them staring right back. So we go on:

> Ere I to school returned
> That dreary time, ere I had been ten days
> A dweller in my Father's house, he died,
> And I and my two Brothers, orphans then,
> Followed his body to the grave. The event
> With all the sorrow which it brought appeared
> A chastisement, and when I called to mind
> That day so lately passed when from the crag
> I looked in such anxiety of hope,
> With trite reflections of morality
> Yet with the deepest passion I bowed low
> To God, who thus corrected my desires.

There is nothing in the original descriptions of the scene to call forth any chastisement, whatever there may have been in the event. The phrase "anxiety of hope," which is all Wordsworth adds thus far to the description, tells too little. The schoolboy became impatient for his father to come that day; he was hoping for a rich holiday experience which he then felt cheated out of; perhaps he was glad his father died and needed to be chastised for *something* because he could not face that pleasure—the moment one starts to imagine, there's no stopping.

What I cannot imagine, though, is that Wordsworth knows something he is not telling, or that he thinks the experience is perfectly clear and his readers should find it so. Thus far, we can say that Wordsworth's mind may have made his outward sense its obedient servant but not that the mind is herein lord and master. Then:

> And afterwards the wind, and sleety rain
> And all the business of the elements,
> The single sheep, and the one blasted tree,
> And the bleak music of that old stone wall,
> The noise of wood and water, and the mist
> Which on the line of each of those two roads
> Advanced in such indisputable shapes . . .

Especially when compared to the sequence beneath the beacon, where the details are ringingly the same whether they be of

126

"ordinary sight" or "visionary dreariness," the details here as he remembers them are different enough from those "as it happened" for us to take note: the sheep and hawthorn that were "companions" are now "The single sheep, and the one blasted tree"; "bleak music" and "noise" are introduced; the mist that "Gave intermitting prospect of the wood / And plain beneath" here advances in "indisputable shapes" along the lines of the two roads. Nothing hallucinatory or visionary, but different in detail and in feeling given to detail.

After this event, to which importance has been attached because Wordsworth connected it to his father's death but which otherwise does not yield much, Wordsworth concludes a great deal:

> All these were spectacles and sounds to which
> I often would repair, and thence would drink
> As at a fountain, and I do not doubt
> That in this later time when storm and rain
> Beat on my roof at midnight, or by day
> When I am in the woods, unknown to me
> The workings of my spirit thence are brought.

Thus far I have quoted from the 1799 *Prelude*; I now add the brief passage which immediately follows the 1805 version of this episode:

> Thou wilt not languish here, O Friend, for whom
> I travel in these dim uncertain ways;
> Thou wilt assist me as a pilgrim gone
> In quest of highest truth. Behold me then
> Once more in Nature's presence, thus restored
> Or otherwise, and strengthened once again
> (With memory left of what had been escaped)
> To habits of devoutest sympathy.

"O mystery of man," Wordsworth had exclaimed after contemplating all he made of the scene below Penrith beacon; here, the exclamation gone, he is much more subdued, and uncertain what he can claim. A pilgrim, yes, in quest of highest truth, but the ways he has just traveled are dim, and he advises Coleridge not to languish there. He is now restored and, for all his claim that his memory of waiting for the horses could be drunk from "as at a fountain," is strengthened "with memory left of what had been escaped," as though the memory could have been lost. *Such a puzzling writer*, and perhaps it was because these lines puzzled even him that he cut them from the 1850 *Prelude*.

Wordsworth feels something of the strangeness we feel, and he is unnerving because he lets so much pile up unexplained and makes no move to help us out: how did the waiting for the horses get attached to his father's death; how does memory recall the scene differently, or, more simply, why are the two descriptions of it different; how can any memory of the scene, summoned or unsummoned, work to restore and strengthen? David Ellis aligns this passage with those of the drowned man and the Winander boy: Wordsworth's imagination transforms something that is dead, or that fears death, into something alive and even serene. I hope I can locate my sense of Wordsworth's strangeness by saying that Ellis' description seems to me both perceptive and unnecessary. Wordsworth himself is the pioneer, and if he is willing to leave his experience puzzling, and even to rejoice in it as it puzzles, why then not delineate the mystery and be content to leave it unsolved?

In a place, a place we can still find, something happened, and a process began. Others have stolen boats, seen graves, or waited in an anxiety of hope, yet have not found in the memory of such experiences a virtue that fructifies or restores—have not experienced a discipline that makes us recognize a grandeur in the beatings of the heart. In that sense what happened after the episodes is at least as important as the episodes themselves, and the process which leads to a restoring virtue is honored in Wordsworth's willingness to allow his accounts of the experiences to remain enigmatic.

We may remember that at one point in "Tintern Abbey" Wordsworth elides his experience of the Wye valley in 1793 with the experiences of his boyhood. Something like that happens in his recollection of the events of the spots of time and his writing of them in Goslar. "The hiding-places of my power," he writes in the 1805 *Prelude,* "Seem open; I approach, and then they close." But there is no suggestion in the 1799 *Prelude* that he felt *then* that the hiding places of his power closed as he approached them, and the virtues that *fructify* in 1798–99 only *vivify* in 1805. The later poet changes the verb, and surely looks on his earlier self—the boy of 1775 or 1783, the poet of 1798–99—with something like nostalgia. "I see by glimpses now," he writes in 1805, and it is in full knowledge of this that he accepts both what has happened to him—and if that was puzzling, why then it was—and his first written accounts of it. If he no longer agreed with what he concluded there, he would change nothing now. On this account we can say that Wordsworth felt he had lost, or was losing, his power the moment he finished his first recording of the discovery of the sources of that power. Childhood ended for him after he invented it.

Given all I have said of Part I of the two-part 1799 *Prelude,* there is little need to dwell on Part II, which, without much altering or rearranging, became the Book II of 1805 and 1850. Most of it was written in Sockburn, and its closing hail and farewell to Coleridge was composed after their walking tour of the Lakes, when Coleridge was going back to London and Wordsworth was returning to get his sister. Part II has a flavor of a more social Wordsworth than the solitary of Part I, as though he were trying to move from love of nature toward love of man. But the record gives the lie to the effort and keeps uncovering, in the midst of society, lovely moments when he is solitary, as when listening to the wren's song in Furness Abbey or to his friend play the flute on an island in Windermere, or when he starts to describe his friendship with a schoolmate, John Fleming, but soon veers off into a moment when he is alone on a jutting eminence, feeling a holy calm spread over his soul. One can hardly say Wordsworth felt no love of others or had no liking for society; rather, those feelings and experiences had less charge for him, and he could not stay interested in describing his youthful experiences with other people.

What the end of Part II shows is that by the time of the move to Grasmere even the tie to Coleridge, the dependence on Coleridge, the need for Coleridge as a catalyst for his poetry, is less than it had been:

> Fare thee well!
> Health and the quiet of a healthful mind
> Attend thee! seeking oft the haunts of men
> But yet more often living with thyself
> And for thyself, so haply shall thy days
> Be many and a blessing to mankind.—

The two had been apart for most of a year, and Wordsworth clearly was feeling the state of being he here wishes for Coleridge. He knew he could write while living alone with Dorothy, and if he consciously felt anything like the trust he had shown as a poet in the previous months, he had no reason to need the presence of anyone else. Increasingly he was feeling, both because of all he had done in Germany and because he was back in England and ready to settle, there was a blessing in the gentle breeze for him. So in all his relations with Coleridge from this point on, it is Coleridge who comes to Wordsworth—coming, indeed, to live some years later—not the other way around.

The first poem Wordsworth wrote after moving to Grasmere was "The Brothers," which is based on a story he heard while walking with Coleridge. It announces from its opening lines that we are in a different place from those described in the 1799 *Prelude*; we are in the Lake District as it had been "discovered" in Wordsworth's lifetime:

> These Tourists, Heaven preserve us! needs must live
> A profitable life: some glance along,
> Rapid and gay, as if the earth were air,
> And they were butterflies to wheel about
> Long as their summer lasted; some, as wise,
> Upon the forehead of a jutting crag
> Sit perched with book and pencil on their knee,
> And look and scribble, scribble on and look,
> Until a man might travel twelve stout miles,
> Or reap an acre of his neighbour's corn.

130

Thus the priest of Ennerdale comments to his wife. Wordsworth himself loved to walk twelve stout miles, but he also loved to scribble and look, likely as not when perched on the forehead of a jutting crag. He was not a shepherd, nor a village priest either, but he could always feel superior to sightseeing tourists in Cumberland and Westmoreland. This opening is followed by a tale that offers place as lore, the priest acting a bit like Evan Dhu in *Waverley*, so that we find out why there are no gravestones in Ennerdale and how the people there take care of an orphan. Wordsworth, clearly, is seeing the place as a place, as he never does in the 1799 *Prelude*. (In the 1805 *Prelude* Wordsworth put in some little guidebook touches, such as the tale of the murderer's name in the scene below Penrith beacon and the name of the place where he stole the boat.)

"The Brothers" was soon followed by "Home at Grasmere," an effusion that begins by claiming so much for Grasmere and for William and Dorothy's life there that soon it gets into trouble by having to hedge on its own claims. What marks its poetry and its sense of place is the imperviousness of Grasmere to what happens there. It is all externally perceived, and as unlike the childhood scenes in *The Prelude* as can be imagined:

> Embrace me, then, ye Hills, and close me in,
> Now in the clear and open day I feel
> Your guardianship; I take it to my heart;
> 'Tis like the solemn shelter of the night.
> But I would call thee beautiful, for mild,
> And soft, and gay, and beautiful thou art,
> Dear Valley, having in thy face a smile
> Though peaceful, full of gladness . . .
> 'Tis (but I cannot name it) 'tis the sense
> Of majesty, and beauty, and repose,
> A blended holiness of earth and sky,
> Something that makes this individual Spot,
> This small abiding-place of many men,
> A termination, and a last retreat,
> A Centre, come from whereso'er you will,
> A Whole without dependence or defect,

Made for itself, and happy in itself,
Perfect Contentment, Unity entire.

This is *winter*, in the Lakes, and less than a hundred lines later Wordsworth mentions there had been "Two months unwearied of severest storm" that "put the temper of our minds to proof." As I noted before, Wordsworth proved himself incapable of describing Grasmere in wild, or haunting or haunted, terms. *That* was all for childhood, for spots of time, and was, he seems to have hoped, all behind him.

"Home at Grasmere" reads like an advertisement in its unawareness of any human life not seen in the most glowing terms: we went there and we just fell in love with the place. William and Dorothy were "A pair seceding from the common world." Whatever the truth of Coleridge's statement that the Wordsworths would never leave the north because they were loved by the people there, with whom they shared a common speech and pronunciation, Wordsworth in his first ecstasy insists that happiness is not people but place, an eventless and peopleless Eden, an extension of Wordsworth's sense of his own power, his own foundness. *He* is his own center, he is whole, so *it* is "unity entire," whatever that may mean.

"Home at Grasmere" presumably was to be part of *The Recluse*, perhaps the opening; consequently Wordsworth had to try to make it philosophical. To do that, however, he had to retreat: he and Dorothy were not after all "seceding from the common world"; Grasmere was not a place so special that only he and Dorothy could feel its grandeur; Grasmere had plenty of human suffering, so that "Man, Nature, and Society" could be examined as well from there as anywhere. After relating some stories of suffering, he retracts and insists, "if I . . . / Am sometimes forced to cast a painful look / Upon unwelcome things," still "The more I see the more is my delight." The poem finally got so tangled that Wordsworth had to drop it, and in effect to drop *The Recluse* with it, though that he could not begin to admit.

Needless to say I do not believe a word of Wordsworth's claims for Grasmere, and doubt he believed many of them for very long. But the contrast between this Grasmere and the places nearer the outlines of the triangle in the 1799 *Prelude*, which is not simply a matter of feeling but of the way places are known, is so great that it becomes an important part of my story. Early in "Home at Grasmere" he offers this contrast between his present and his past:

> What I keep, have gained,
> Shall gain, must gain, if sound be my belief
> From past and present, rightly understood,
> That in my day of childhood I was less
> The mind of Nature, less, take all in all,
> Whatever may be lost, than I am now.
> For proof behold this Valley, and behold
> Yon Cottage, where with me my Emma dwells.

This passage barely makes sense without *The Prelude*, where Wordsworth had first written about what he was, or what "the mind of Nature" was in his "day of childhood." Without that reference we would have no notion of what he has weighed with what when he concludes that "all in all" he was less then than he is now. Nor, if we bear in mind the 1805 *Prelude* passage about the closing of the hiding places of his power, or the faded gleam of the Intimations Ode, can it be said that the assessment offered here lasted. But in "Tintern Abbey" there is a nagging because unspecified phrase about Wordsworth's having received "abundant recompense" for a loss sustained over the years, and of course we do have the 1799 *Prelude* and can surmise that he uncovered or created a huge respect for his day of childhood while writing it.

In his moving to Grasmere, in his discovering there a home for life, in the effusions of "Home at Grasmere," Wordsworth seems at least a little bit more

> like a man
> Flying from something that he dreads, than one
> Who sought the thing he loved.

In his first year there, in addition to "The Brothers" and "Home at Grasmere," he wrote the five poems "on the naming of places," and "Rural Architecture," "The Childless Father," the Derwentwater hermitage "Inscription," "Some have died for love," "The Oak and the Broom," "The Waterfall and the Eglantine," "The Two Thieves," "The Idle Shepherd Boys," and "Michael." All are poems about places in and around Grasmere, or are stories and lore local to the area. Then, having done this strenuous poetic settling into his new home, he stashed these poems into the second edition of *Lyrical Ballads* and never again wrote about Grasmere as a place.

In moving to Grasmere Wordsworth put his winter in Goslar into the background, and with it the 1799 *Prelude* and his childhood. Now he was creating a second "home," a second Lake District. One must scour the detailed compilations of Mark Reed's chronology to see if, even once in the next fifty years, he ever returned to the places of his haunted youth. As he writes about it, Grasmere could be in a different country instead of at the heart of the triangle, its glowing tones so sharply contrasting with those used to create the height above Penrith or the hill above the converging roads outside Hawkshead. (For what it is worth, we know from *The Prelude* that Wordsworth did revisit the Penrith beacon in 1788 or 1789, and in later years Wordsworth stopped in Penrith on his way over the Pennines, but there is no mention of his returning to the beacon after he recreated it as the first spot of time.)

In 1804–5 Wordsworth went back to *The Prelude*, first expanding it to five books and then to thirteen. The great new ingredient in the 1805 *Prelude*, in addition to the accounts of life in Cambridge, London, and France during the Revolution, is "imagination." The term serves so many functions and bears such shifting relations to the other human faculties, to Nature, and to God—matters that have been thoroughly examined—that it is not possible now to make a simple responsible statement about it. Fortunately, here I can restrict myself to asking what happened to Wordsworth's sense of his childhood after he cut himself off from its places. The next question is how the 1805 *Prelude* deals with the places, brought in from the 1799 poem intact, though Wordsworth himself is a very different person and poet.

Wordsworth made two famous statements, both dating from

March 1802, about his relation to his childhood. The first is "The Rainbow":

> My heart leaps up when I behold
>     A Rainbow in the sky:
> So was it when my life began;
> So is it now I am a Man;
> So be it when I shall grow old,
>     Or let me die!
> The Child is Father of the Man;
> And I could wish my days to be
> Bound each to each by natural piety.

In "Tintern Abbey," whatever Wordsworth lost in ceasing to be a child, he finds "abundant recompense"; in "Home at Grasmere," "take all in all," he is more now as a man than he was as a child. But in "The Rainbow," the best the man, young or old, can achieve is something he had as a child, and adult life is not imagined to yield any more and perhaps will not continue to yield as much. The child that is father of the man, as David Ferry pointed out years ago, has the advantage of the man regardless of whether it is better to be a father or a child.

The first four sections of the Intimations Ode were begun the same week as "The Rainbow," and build into high lament the feeling that "The things which I have seen I now can see no more." If "natural piety" is what binds the man to the child, the Ode knows that that is not glue enough, and that the light of "our life's Star," like the colors of the rainbow, must pass "into the light of common day." In neither of these poems is childhood represented as taking place in specific locations, but we might have expected as much after the move to Grasmere and the change in the way the places are rendered. What is surprising about the Ode is how it transforms the major facts of Wordsworth's childhood as the 1799 *Prelude* understood and specified them. Here he tells of a time of light, joy, new-born blisses, Mother's kisses, and light from Father's eyes, all of which his early years may have contained, and all of which, it might be claimed, are appropriate to a mythologizing of childhood. But we know that the 1799 *Prelude* was right, and so did the Wordsworth who changed so little of his first descriptions of childhood experience in his reworkings of *The Prelude*. What the earlier poem shows is that, however great the joys, however pleasant much of the routine of family and social life, the deepest experiences were not light but dark and fearful, because in those experiences he was most deeply touched by the animate powers of places, the deities of hills and sky. That the verse in the Ode about childhood is strained and sentimental is evidence enough that Wordsworth "knew" this, and having allowed himself such falsifying, he blithely moves into deep waters indeed when he makes the leap from lyric cry—"But yet I know, where'er I go"— to generalizations that attempt to speak for all of us—"Our birth is but a sleep and a forgetting."

The simple sequence of events from 1798 on as experienced by the adult goes like this: after a particularly difficult and isolated winter in Germany, Wordsworth returns to England, uncertain of where he and Dorothy would settle; the fortunate happenstance of Coleridge's visiting north and their walking in the Lake District draws him to Grasmere, where he soon sets up house and falls into precisely the kind of routine he and Dorothy had always longed for; soon after getting over an initial rapturous falling in love with home at Grasmere, he marries happily and begins a family, knowing his way of life need never in its essentials alter again. But even as his life was achieving this shape, he knew he was moving away from something he once had and now envied. There may be a note of loss in that unattached "abundant recompense" in "Tintern Abbey," but there is none in the 1799 *Prelude*. There childhood had place, it had action and feelings attached to places, it had terror—and there the childhood is as little lost as can be imagined. The adult faces the child, trusts the child's experience, and in making poetry of that trust achieves as much of abundant recompense as can be achieved, given that the past is past. The places of childhood power had opened, and *then* they had not closed.

In Grasmere Wordsworth changed his terms, changed his way of describing places, and took all place, action, and clarity out of his allusions to or descriptions of his childhood. He had the life he wanted and could hardly be expected to believe that the poetry of 1802 and after could never be as good as that of 1798–99. He had a great deal of poetic power left, as the 1805 *Prelude* shows, but he had lost the relation of childhood experience to adult poetry about that experience, given up adult trust in childhood place. The Intimations Ode therefore beautifully conveys a sense of loss even as it also falsifies what had been lost:

> while the sun shines warm,
> And the Babe leaps up on his mother's arm:—
>  I hear, I hear, with joy I hear!
>  —But there's a Tree, of many one,
> A single Field which I have looked upon,
> Both of them speak of something that is gone ...

In the contrived stridency of the "I hear, I hear, with joy I hear," there is implicit admission that there was something specious in the rapturousness of "Home at Grasmere"; in that tree and that field we have something like that poem's true end.

Early in 1804 Wordsworth read Part II of the 1799 *Prelude* aloud to Coleridge, presumably for the first time, and that seems to have turned him back to his "poem about my life," and indeed back to writing at all after a relatively inactive 1803. A few weeks later, he wrote that "now after a long sleep" he was busily engaged in turning the 1799 poem into a five-part poem. The first three books, as projected, were approximately the ones that emerged in the 1805 *Prelude*; Book IV was to contain parts of what became IV-V; and Book V was to include the spots of time and the climbing of Mount Snowden. Almost as soon as he finished the poem he had outlined, Wordsworth dismantled it, and a year and a half later finished the thirteen-book *Prelude* of 1805. As I noted before, most of the language in the first *Prelude* is in later versions, though some is rearranged and much is given a different context. Once Wordsworth had turned from his childhood places and experiences and implicitly thereby from the 1799 *Prelude*, for him to return to that poem, and to realize that it had to be kept intact, would have been like King Saul's insisting to the witch whose witchcraft he himself had outlawed that she summon the one figure, Samuel, who would most condemn him. The 1799 *Prelude* shows how much the Intimations Ode had distorted Wordsworth's childhood, and it bears an uneasy relation to those new parts of the 1805 *Prelude* that stress the supreme power of imagination and the growth of the poet's mind. His childhood experiences show Wordsworth as passive, and becoming receptive principally through the agency of fear. Hence the role played by the imagination, even when one stretches the term and its powers, must be seen as secondary in the boyhood experiences, while the role played by the intervening and disciplining powers inherent in places is necessarily prominent. The past had to be honored by leaving alone what he had written. He thereby acknowledged that he could never again write about places as he had written about them at Goslar, and that what he could not explain in 1798–99 he had better not try to explain now, regardless of the high reaches he now claimed for the imagination. So the major task in 1804–5, in the thirteen-book *Prelude* and in the final seven parts to the Intimations Ode, was to ensure that he was nonetheless all right, thanks to the power of imagination and the "years that bring the philosophic mind."

Let us go back to the passage which Wordsworth added in 1804–5 to the first spot of time. He tells us that when he returned to the scene with Mary Hutchinson, it was not to feel the childhood terror, but "The spirit of pleasure and youth's golden gleam" made even more radiant by "these remembrances, and from the power / They left behind." Wordsworth is amazed:

> Oh! mystery of Man, from what a depth
> Proceed thy Honours! I am lost, but see
> In simple childhood something of the base
> On which thy greatness stands; but this I feel,
> That from thyself it is that thou must give,
> Else never canst receive.

Wordsworth does not say what it was the boy gave that enabled the man to receive later. The closest I can come is to say that, at age five or six, then again at age seventeen or eighteen, and then finally at age twenty-nine when he first wrote of the spots of time, he gave by *not* explaining, by not letting the mind be lord and master in a governing, interpreting way. He is awed by what he had done:

> The days gone by
> Come back upon me from the dawn almost
> Of life: the hiding-places of my power
> Seem open; I approach, and then they close;
> I see by glimpses now; when age comes on,
> May scarcely see at all, and I would give,
> While yet we may, as far as words can give,
> A substance and a life to what I feel:
> I would enshrine the spirit of the past
> For future restoration.

He might not have been able to write as he once had written, but he knew it, and, for me at least, these lines are worth a dozen odes.

The hiding places of power were open in 1798–99, and they closed to the point of being visible only in glimpses by 1804–5, in part because he had closed them in his move to Grasmere and his creation of his second "home" in the Lake District. If there are only glimpses now, and the process is irreversible, what is left is not the philosophic mind, or thoughts that lie too deep for tears, but a shoring up against the ruin. There is that puzzling shift from "*I* would give" to "While yet *we* may," and the best I can do to explain it is to guess that the "future restoration" will come not by means of his remembering the childhood experience but by our reading his poetry.

What he thought he could do, what he hoped he could do, beyond that, is expressed in a representative anecdote in the passage describing the climbing of Snowden. Judgments about this passage (XIII, 1-119, in the 1805 *Prelude*) differ widely, and it will come as no surprise if I say it seems to me a jigsaw puzzle scene in which all the pieces fit neatly, a composed landscape in which the loss of the hiding places of power is supposedly recompensed abundantly. I admit to thinking of this as the climbing of Mount Fuji, as seen in a Japanese landscape painting:

When at my feet the ground appeared to brighten,
And with a step or two seemed brighter still;
Nor had I time to ask the cause of this,
For instantly a Light upon the turf
Fell like a flash: I looked about, and lo!
The Moon stood naked in the Heavens, at height
Immense above my head, and on the shore
I found myself of a huge sea of mist,
Which, meek and silent, rested at my feet.
A hundred hills their dusky backs upheaved
All over this still Ocean, and beyond,
Far, far beyond, the vapours shot themselves,
In headlands, tongues, and promontory shapes,
Into the Sea, the real Sea, that seemed
To dwindle and give up its majesty,
Usurped upon as far as sight could reach.

It is a scene, a Thomson scene, and whatever the experience had been in 1791, in 1804–5 it is all turned into emblems of beauty and authority. Not only was the experience breathtaking, but in climbing out of darkness and into unexpected light he was also given an external symbol of his having climbed, and got above the clouds.

The problem is that we know it is being offered as a climactic experience, and there are telltale signs in the description that Wordsworth is going to insist on arranging it so that it is not just a breathtaking scene. Thus the mist is "meek and silent," and yet is powerful enough to make "the real Sea" "give up its majesty," thereby establishing a hierarchy created not by nature but by the observer. Next,

　　　　　　　　　　　from the shore
At distance not the third part of a mile
Was a blue chasm; a fracture in the vapour,
A deep and gloomy breathing-place, through which
Mounted the roar of waters, torrents, streams
Innumerable, roaring with one voice.
The universal spectacle throughout

Was shaped for admiration and delight,
Grand in itself alone, but in that breach
Through which the homeless voice of waters rose,
That dark deep thoroughfare had Nature lodged
The Soul, the Imagination of the whole.

Compare this with any of the great childhood scenes in *The Prelude* and you see precisely how convenient, how arranged, how totally unmysterious it all is. The moment the adult becomes nature's, or God's, partner, this sense of convenience and arrangement is almost bound to arise. The child's mind as lord and master, the poet of the childhood places as lord and master, is so much stranger, so much more like a real mind experiencing something really powerful, than this cardboard scene. Here on Mount Snowden we are on our way to Shelley's "Mont Blanc" and Tennyson's "The Palace of Art."

As I have written elsewhere, the nineteenth century is Wordsworth's century because from him flows that great stream of literature that shapes life by shaping a relation of childhood to place, in the work of the Brontës, Dickens, George Eliot, Hardy, and Lawrence, to name only major examples. But I hope the story I have been telling shows more than this. It is not for nothing that Wordsworth is, along with Coleridge, the decisive inaugurating spirit of English Romanticism. I hope I have helped make clear why these fifty years of great change are distorted when thought of simply as the Romantic period, distorted in the neglect of writers as various and impressive as Crabbe, Cobbett, and Clare and in the underrating of Austen's historical achievement and originality. The matter need not rest there, however, at least not yet.

The "O mystery of man" lines at the end of the first spot of time are one of two great passages Wordsworth added in 1804–5 when reading over his 1798–99 work and contemplating his early years. The other is the passage in Book III that begins

O Heavens! how awful is the might of Souls,
And what they do within themselves, while yet

> The yoke of earth is new to them, the world
> Nothing but a wide field where they were sown.

It is a long way from here to Jane Eyre in the Red Room, Maggie Tulliver covering her hurt by running to the gypsies, Pip brooding on his sister's having brought him up by jerks, Heathcliff and Cathy standing outside Thrushcross Grange, Jude peering toward Christminster, Paul Morel praying that his father would, and would not, die. The novelists wonderfully describe childhood experience etching and shaping lives, but their people are ordinary people, and their places are, in truth, ordinary sights. Here we have "the might of Souls," which Wordsworth goes on to call his "heroic argument" because it is "empires" we inherit "as natural beings in the strength of Nature." Wordsworth, thus, not only was shaped by his childhood, but in crucial moments was given, or experienced, the power that destined him to be great, and this is more than anyone wants to claim for Jane, Maggie, Pip, Heathcliff, Cathy, Jude, or Paul.

We can see this insistence on the hiding places of power and the might of youthful souls as Wordsworth's attempt to claim for himself the ancient bardic role of poet and for his experience a grandeur as complete as any that might be claimed for Achilles or Aeneas. Unless he could make that claim for *The Prelude*, he would have to chastise himself deeply for not going on with *The Recluse*, to say nothing of not writing of the fall of princes and the fate of nations. But in making the claim that his novelistic successors would never make for their characters nor the characters for themselves, Wordsworth has been a model, and not just for poets, in the eras that followed. From him we derive our sense that an individual's experience is by itself material enough for great poetry, and he shows how poetry can be made where no poetry had been, and where few models for it existed.

The consequences of this Wordsworthian experience can be named in many ways. More than anyone else, Wordsworth is responsible for our cultivation of originality, not just in the language of poetry but in experiencing the life that offers material for the poetry. He also shows how, in his own case over a period of forty-five years, one can wrestle, and fail, and finally

142

give up wrestling with the powers that seemed inherent in one-self and in one's experiences when young. Wordsworth's way of showing how failure is the price of greatness has been our way in the last two centuries. He did not, in his years of decline, offer a very "romantic" image of failure—Shelley made him into the ultra-legitimately dull Peter Bell the Third with reason, and one could never call Wordsworth's life romantic or exciting. But what he did not supply—the life that fell into colorful excess—is unimportant compared to his dedication to his own experience as the stuff of great poetry.

Other writers, who themselves may have felt they were given powers similar to Wordsworth's, have then had to struggle to be or not be like him, or as original as he was. But the rest of us, feeling no such struggle, can feel something else, the large human power that lies in Wordsworth's opening of himself, trusting of himself, and thereby understanding the mysteriousness of himself. If I am uncertain about the presence of grandeur in the beating of my heart, in Wordsworth's enacting of the relation of power to acceptance and trust, of giving in order to receive, there is for me or anyone a sense of restoration. Like all models in the two centuries of the real, the local, and the particular, this is a non-teaching or at least non-prescribing one. Wordsworth's way of being open involves his first home, amid crags and slopes and lakes, where place is enshrined as the vehicle of power; it also involves his having trusted that the experience would guide the poet, and the later poet's having trusted the younger poet. Out of this trust came great poetry, but out of it also came virtue, fruitful, enlivening, restoring. And for such an example anyone might well be grateful.

# ❧ REFERENCES

## 1. CIRCUMSTANCES ALTER OCCASIONS

Imlac on the poet comes in *Rasselas,* Ch. X; Keats on the making of souls comes near the end of his long letter to George and Georgiana Keats, February 14–May 3, 1819.

For a full report on Fawley and *Jude the Obscure,* see my "In Hardy Country," *New York Review of Books,* June 23, 1977, pp. 41–44.

Duncan and Banquo on Inverness Castle is in *Macbeth,* I, 6, 1–9.

The opening lines of "To Penshurst" are quoted from Ben Jonson, *The Complete Poems,* ed. George Parfitt (New Haven, 1975); the prospect from Hagley Park is quoted from James Thomson, *The Poetical Works,* ed. J. Logie Robertson (London, 1961), "Spring," 950–962.

John Barrell, *The Idea of Landscape and the Sense of Place* (Cambridge, 1972) is a valuable book; on "visual / pictorial," p. 1; on Thomson's Hagley Park, pp. 12–20.

The passages from *The Task* are quoted from *The Poetical Works of William Cowper,* ed. H. S. Milford (London, 1959), I, 150–153, 163–179.

The works on Constable are Michael Rosenthal, *John Constable* (New Haven, 1983), pp. 124–132, and John Barrell, *The Dark Side of the Landscape* (Cambridge, 1980), pp. 146–147. On "The Hay Wain," see Alistair Smart and Altfield Brooks, *Constable and His Country* (London, 1976).

145

## 2. GEORGE CRABBE

The standard edition of Crabbe's poems is still the one by A. C. Ward (Cambridge, 1905); the passages quoted from "The Village" are 63–78 and 252–239; from "Peter Grimes," which is Letter XXII of *The Borough*, 171–180, 181–195; 202–204; 209–216; 240–244, and 298–313; from the preface to *Tales in Verse*, vol. II, p. 6; from "Arabella," 9–10, 23–28, 41, 225–226, and 325–326; from "The Widow's Tale," 19–26, 76–83, 124, 127, 333–334, 415–423.

F. R. Leavis on Crabbe is in *Revaluation* (London, 1936), pp. 124–129; Ezra Pound on Crabbe is in *Literary Essays* (Norfolk, Conn., 1954), p. 279; Jane Austen's letter about Crabbe and Miss Lee is in *Letters 1796–1817*, ed. R. W. Chapman (London, 1955).

## 3. JANE AUSTEN

All quotations are from R. W. Chapman's standard edition (Oxford, 1923) in five volumes (each title subdivided into "volumes" and chapters, here in parentheses), as follows: *Northanger Abbey*, V, "Does our education" (II, ix); *Pride and Prejudice*, II, "They gradually ascended" and "The introduction, however," (both III, i); *Mansfield Park*, III, "The politeness which" (I, ix), "Here's harmony" (I, xi), "If any one faculty" (II, iv), "Have you any reason, child" (III, i); *Emma*, IV, "Their road" (I, x), "Much could not be hoped" (II, ix), "How is your niece" (II, x); *Persuasion*, V, "Anne had not wanted" (I, vi). Chapman's comments on Pemberley and on the ostensible moral of *Mansfield Park* are in *Jane Austen: Facts and Problems* (Oxford, 1949), p. 192 and p. 194. D. W. Harding's "Regulated Hatred" first appeared in *Scrutiny*, 8 (1940), 346–362. Lionel Trilling's essay on *Mansfield Park* is in *The Opposing Self* (New York, 1955), pp. 206–230. Mary Mitford on Austen's villages is in *Our Village* (Everyman edition, n.d.), p. 2. Raymond Williams on Austen's communities is in *The City and the Country* (Oxford, 1973), p. 166. Ronald Blythe calls *Emma* the Parthenon of fiction in his introduction to the Penguin English Library edition, and Marvin Mudrick calls Austen "world champion novelist" in *Nobody Here But Us Chickens* (New Haven and New York, 1981), p. 172.

## 4. WILLIAM COBBETT

All quotations from *Rural Rides* are from the one edition currently in print, in the Penguin English Library, ed. George Woodcock (London, 1967); references are by the date of the ride as well as by page number: "I took Richard" (October 30, 1825, pp. 251–254); "The people dirty, poor-looking" (September 4, 1823, p. 206); "Here is a hill" (September 3, 1823, pp. 199–200); "Oak clothes-chests" (October 20, 1825, pp. 226–227); "These hills are amongst the most barren" (August 5, 1823, p. 139); "I found the place *altered*" (August 30, 1826, p. 321).

Wordsworth's sonnet is quoted from Stephen Gill's Oxford Authors *Wordsworth*.

The sentences from E. P. Thompson on the changes in our period is from his classic *The Making of the English Working Class* (Harmondsworth, 1980), p. 209.

## 5. JOHN CLARE

Except for the quotations from "To the Violet" and "Ballad," which are quoted from John Clare, *Selected Poems*, ed. J. W. and Anne Tibble (London, 1979), all quotations from Clare's poetry are from *The Midsummer Cushion*, ed. Anne Tibble and R. K. R. Thornton (Northumberland and Manchester, 1979). Because this volume is disappearing, let me note that many poems from this edition, and a generous selection of all Clare's poems, are currently available in the Oxford Authors *John Clare* (Oxford, 1984), ed. Eric Robinson and David Powell.

The passages from Clare's prose are from *Autobiographical Writings*, ed. Eric Robinson (Oxford, 1983), p. 34, p. 53; Clare on *The Village Minstrel* can be found in J. W. and Anne Tibble, *John Clare, His Life and Poetry* (London, 1956), p. 84; on Crabbe, in *The Letters of John Clare*, ed. the Tibbles (London, 1951), p. 75; on Wordsworth, *The Letters of John Clare*, p. 133.

John Barrell on Clare, "It may be that the particularly," is in *New Pelican Guide to English Literature*, ed. Boris Ford (Harmondsworth, 1982), V, pp. 233–234; subsequent quotations are from *The Idea of Landscape and the Sense of Place* (Cambridge, 1972), pp. 172, 173, 188.

## 6. WILLIAM WORDSWORTH

I quote from *The Prelude 1798–1799*, ed. Stephen Parrish (Ithaca, 1977), as follows: from the JJ Notebook, Fragments $X^v$ and $Y^r$, 64–79, and Fragment $X^r$, 111–117; from Parrish's reading text of the completed poem, I, 331–349, 349–360, 361–367, 368–374; II, 509–514. All other quotations are from the Oxford Authors *William Wordsworth* (Oxford, 1984), ed. Stephen Gill, as follows: "Home at Grasmere," 338–341, 693, 129–136, 161–170, 91–98; "Tintern Abbey," 69–73, 73–76; "The Brothers," 1–10; the 1805 *Prelude*, XI, 390–397, 329–334, 334–343, XIII, 36–51, 54–65; III, 178–181. Gill's claim about the chronology of his edition is on p. v.

Jonathan Wordsworth is quoted from his *The Borders of Vision* (Oxford, 1982), pp. vii–viii.

Wordsworth's letter to Dorothy on settling in Grasmere is in *The Letters of William and Dorothy Wordsworth*, ed. Ernest de-Selincourt (Oxford, 1967), and was written November 8, 1799; hers to an unknown recipient was written in 1799, otherwise undated.

David Ellis' work is *Wordsworth, Freud, and the Spots of Time* (Cambridge and New York, 1985); Geoffrey Hartman on the many changes in a passage in Book VI of *The Prelude* is in his *Wordsworth's Poetry 1787–1814* (New Haven, 1964), pp. 203–207. My earlier account of Wordsworth is in *Literary Inheritance* (Amherst, 1984), pp. 107–154.

## 🕭 INDEX